Dave Doroghy | Graeme Menzies

111 Places
in Victoria
That You Must
Not Miss

(**111**)

emons:

To Jeannie, who opened up
my eyes to this amazing city.
Dave Doroghy

To John Lennon. Sorry I couldn't
include your Rolls-Royce.
Graeme Menzies

© Emons Verlag GmbH
All rights reserved
© Photographs by Dave Doroghy and Graeme Menzies, except see p. 238
© Cover Icon: Istockphoto.com/raclros
Layout: Editorial Design & Art Direction, Conny Laue,
based on a design by Lübbeke | Naumann | Thoben
Maps: altancicek.design, www.altancicek.de
Basic cartographical information from Openstreetmap,
© OpenStreetMap-Mitwirkende, OdbL
Editing: Karen E. Seiger
Printing and binding: Grafisches Centrum Cuno, Calbe
Printed in Germany 2023
ISBN 978-3-7408-1720-6
First edition

Guidebooks for Locals & Experienced Travelers
Join us in uncovering new places around the world at
www.111places.com

Foreword

For decades Victoria has had a nickname that pokes fun at the people who live here. It must drive the folks at Tourism Victoria nuts to hear the place referred to as "the home of newlyweds and nearly deads." But there actually is some truth behind this tongue-in-cheek moniker. A lot of newlyweds really do honeymoon in Victoria. They love the city's endless romantic seaside strolls, fun quirky tourist attractions and great restaurants, bars, cafés and hotels. And a lot of seniors from across Canada really have chosen Victoria for their retirement home, substituting the cold snowy winters of just about everywhere else in the country for Victoria's temperate (if sometimes wet) winters, more gardens than you can shake a bouquet of roses at, and a host of museums, lush golf courses, art galleries, seaside activities, and a laid-back West-Coast vibe that can rejuvenate even the most wearied office warrior.

But writing this third book together – a follow-up to our Vancouver and Whistler guidebooks – we wanted to show there is much more to Victoria than that. As you flip through these pages, we hope you will see that Victoria is home to a wide variety of people and has an equally diverse collection of things to do and places to visit. Many of these places can be part of your own walking tour of downtown Victoria. Some may be more suited to a bike tour. A few will enhance or inspire a road trip slightly beyond the downtown core. All of them – from forgotten forts to funky fences – have been chosen for the many amusing and often surprising stories that shed light on the true and unique character of British Columbia's capital city.

If we have done our job well, you'll agree with us that Victoria is not just for star-struck lovers and energetic retirees. It is a vibrant, interesting, contemporary, and imaginative place that simultaneously embraces and defies its stereotypes. So get out there and start exploring these places in Victoria that you must not miss!

111 Places

1 _ 1994 Commonwealth Games
The missing Inner Harbour stage

Looking out onto Victoria's inner harbour, imagine a large, ornate barge with an Olympic-style, three-level podium as its symbolic centrepiece. It's covered with flags from all the Commonwealth nations and colourful flowers and banners. It has a huge jumbotron video screen. On this stage, every night during the 1994 Commonwealth Games, fireworks would accompany loud patriotic music, as gold, silver, and bronze medals were awarded to the young men and women that competed in different sporting events that day. Thousands of excited spectators seated in the unique horseshoe-shaped harbour's amphitheatre would watch from the rows and rows of temporary seating.

The biggest event in Canada in the 1990s was the Commonwealth Games. 2,500 athletes from 63 nations competed in the 15th edition of these mega multi-disciplinary games, and the competition to stage them was fierce. On September 15th, 1988, after a long bidding process, Victoria beat out New Delhi, India and Cardiff, Wales for the right to host this event that's been held every four years in a different Commonwealth Nation since 1930.

This grandiose and totally unique floating stage was part of an aggressive international bid to bring the games to Victoria. The only problem was that after being awarded them, the Local Organising Committee re-evaluated the costs to fit out and build the floating stage and decided it was cost prohibitive. Despite that part of the plans being eliminated, the games were a huge success and had a transformative effect on the city. Most of the plans did materialise, including an Olympic-sized swimming pool in Saanich and a cycling velodrome in Colwood. For a huge international event of this scope and grandeur, there are no monuments or statues in Victoria to commemorate it, except for this 1 x 1.5 metre (3 x 5 foot) plaque mounted on the south side of the Inner Harbour's stone wall.

XV COMMONWEALTH GAMES · AUGUST 18-28, 1994
XV JEUX DU COMMONWEALTH · AOÛT 18-28, 1994

Address 720 Government Street, Victoria, BC V8V 1A1, www.victoria.ca | Getting there Bus 30, 31, 75 to Legislative Terminal at Belleville | Hours Unrestricted | Tip Look for the illuminated sign nearby with huge letters reading C A N A D A, the largest country in the Commonwealth by size (812 Wharf Street, www.tourismvictoria.com/plan/local-info/visitor-centre).

2 Abkhazi Garden Tea House
Royal tea with royalty

The Abkhazi Garden Tea House was originally built by the last surviving son of an ancient line of kings from the Black Sea. The reasons to visit this home-turned-teahouse are manifold. First of all, you must see the garden. It features natural rocky slopes and native Garry oak trees mixed among Japanese maples, and rhododendrons that have grown to an impressive maturity over the last 80 years, with carpets of heather, irises, and daylilies.

Secondly, think of your stomach. You have feasted your eyes and your nose outdoors – now go into the tea house and let your taste buds get some of the action. Choose from high tea, afternoon tea, elevenses, and lunch. You can order a piece of Abkhazi Garden vegetable quiche, or nibble away on a smoked salmon profiterole with caramelised shallot cream and dill, or you can try a more traditional freshly baked currant scone with housemade clotted cream and homemade preserves.

If history and romance ring your tea bell, then the third reason to visit is a love story. Prince Nicholas Abkhazi was born in Georgia in 1899 but fled to Paris in the early 1920s after his father Konstantin was shot by the Bolsheviks. When World War II broke out, he joined the French Army but was captured and spent several years at a prisoner of war camp in Germany.

Meanwhile, Peggy Pemberton-Carter was born in Shanghai in 1902 and orphaned by age three. She spent the war years of 1943–45 interned by the Japanese. These two lost souls had met briefly in Paris in the 1920s and somehow managed to stay in touch over the years. They eventually reunited in New York, married, and then – after the chaos and tragedy of European revolutions and wars – decided to plant themselves in the peaceful serenity of Victoria. Arriving in 1946, they spent the rest of their days building a life of love, peace, and beauty at this one-acre home.

Address 1964 Fairfield Road, Victoria, BC V8S 1H3, +1 (778) 265-6466, www.abkhaziteahouse.com, info@abkhaziteahouse.com | Getting there Bus 3, 7 to Foul Bay at Fairfield | Hours Apr–Aug daily 11–5pm; Sep–Mar Wed–Sun 11am–4pm | Tip Nearby Gonzales Hill Regional Park offers spectacular views of the area, especially from the Gonzales Observatory building (340 Dennison Road, www.crd.bc.ca).

3 Adirondacks of Kitty Islet
The chairs with the heavenly view

There are not many places where you can get a view like this. And it's not just the view that's spectacular – it's also the place. Kitty Islet is a small island located on the east side of McNeill Bay, easy to overlook, and definitely worth paying a visit.

Although it's just a three-minute walk from Beach Drive, it might as well be a thousand miles away from the worries and stresses of daily life. When you leave the car behind and sink into one of the permanently placed, iconic Adirondack chairs, you might just as well have left the world behind. Sitting on the chairs on a clear day, looking out toward the strait and beyond to the Olympic Mountains, it almost feels as though you have been transported to your own private island.

If someone else has beaten you to the perch, you can simply stroll around a bit and go investigate the rocky bluffs that surround you. They are an equally good place from which to take in the view, do some bird watching, or watch for the occasional sun-tanning sea lion. Kitty Islet is left *au naturelle* and is surrounded by driftwood that changes position with the tides. So be aware that if you visit at high tide, it's going to be a little more challenging to get here.

In between you and the mountains nearby, you can see the Trial Islands. Not only are they an ecological reserve popular with the local wildlife, but they are home to one of the few lighthouses still operated by real people. The first lighthouse there was built in 1906; the one you see today dates from 1970. Bring binoculars for the full effect.

Finally, while taking in these views, you can also take in some history. McNeill Bay is named after William Henry McNeill, captain of the famous Hudson's Bay Company steamship the S.S. *Beaver*. It was at this bay in 1843 that McNeill anchored the *Beaver* while scouting for a suitable place to build Fort Victoria.

Address Across the street from 572 Beach Avenue, Victoria, BC V8S 2M5, www.oakbaytourism.com | **Getting there** Bus 1, 2 to Central at Transit | **Hours** Unrestricted | **Tip** Near the stairs down to Kitty Islet beach, look for the stone cairn featuring artwork by Tsartlip artist Charles Elliott (Temosen), which marks Kitty Islet as the site of a Songhees camp associated with the main village site of Chikawich located further west in the bay (www.burntembers.com/2011/09/24/chikawich-tlikwaynung-cairn).

4__Archer Murals
A giant tribute to Eddie Van Halen

World renowned artist Paul Archer has manifested everything good that's ever happened to him. When he wanted to become a rock-and-roll "roadie," he just showed up at a concert in roadie clothes and long hair and enthusiastically began moving sound equipment. He eventually got hired and ended up becoming a stagehand at the old Victoria Memorial Arena in 1980, which is where he met Eddie Van Halen.

Fast forward four decades, and Archer's track record of making good things happen grew exponentially. The Victoria native went on to paint over 17,000 murals on the sides of buildings throughout Canada, the United States, and the Cayman Islands. His art is amazing, and to say it's everywhere is not an exaggeration. Next time you see an eye-popping, vibrant mural just about anywhere you happen to be, look for his black "Archer" signature in a bottom corner. His domestic contracts over the years have included assignments for Expo 86, the Vancouver International Airport, Nike Canada, and Molson Canadian and Labatt Blue.

With his beloved little dog Lannah, Archer still travels around North America in his van, painting and spreading messages of hope, peace, and optimism wherever they go. And what a long, strange trip it has been. His reputation and fame drew the attention of many celebrities, like Ozzy Osbourne, Rob Zombie, Sarah McLaughlin, and many others who went on to become his friends. He has even met Frank Zappa and his kids.

With all the travelling he does, Archer could have his base of operations just about anywhere, but he keeps his global headquarters in a warehouse space on Fort Street. That's where he painted the two-story, airbrushed tribute to Eddie Van Halen, who died on October 6th, 2020, at the age of 65. The mural took two full days to paint under wet and cold conditions. Archer hopes that the art will honour the rocker and remind people of his talent.

Address 847 Fort Street, Victoria, BC V8W 1H6 (best viewed from the back lane), www.instagram.com/archerairbrushingofficial | **Getting there** Bus 3, 11, 14, 15, 22 to Fort at Quadra | **Hours** Unrestricted | **Tip** Not far from Archer's studio is one of his most recent works of art, a 16-foot-high, black-and-white mural of Wednesday Addams from *The Addams Family*. Appropriately, it was completed on Friday the 13th in January 2023 (850 Broughton Street).

5 Artful Manhole Covers

Remarkable manhole medallions

The City of Victoria has three "site integrated art installations," which provide a practical municipal service as manhole covers. Turn your gaze downwards to look for a turtle design, a moon, and a tribute to a *Yellow Pages* ad from the 1950s.

The *Turtle Medallion* is a rather handsome manhole cover, designed by artist Jerry-Lee Cerny. Her design, in bronze with a greenish patina, adds a very attractive lustre to the corner of Quadra Street and King's Road. The *Moon Medallion* is a remarkable and cheerful work by artist Richard Hunt, better known for his wood carvings than his metal medallions. Internationally recognized for his talent, Hunt, whose indigenous name is Gwel-la-yo-gwe-la-gya-les, was the first Indigenous artist to be inducted into the Order of British Columbia. The third medallion, *Molly's Original Cake Shop,* was created by Robert Wise and Christian Giroux. This one pays tribute to the neighbourhood and its many unique small businesses in the form of an imaginary *Yellow Pages* ad for the type of shop that would have been part of this community in the middle part of the 1900s.

Searching for these manhole medallions is the perfect excuse to visit the Quadra Village area and browse its urban-eclectic collection of shops and businesses. Walk north on Quadra Street, just a little past Hillside Avenue, and you'll find the offices of CKKQ-FM ("The Q"), Victoria's oldest Rock station. The iconic and unusual Roxy Theatre, which operates out of a Quonset hut is located near the medallions, at 2657 Quadra Street, and definitely worth a peek. For retro sign-lovers, the Sparkle Bright Launderette at 2584 Quadra has a classic vintage sign outside, likely dating from when it opened in the 1960s. If you want to be as eclectic as the neighbourhood, bring some tracing paper and a crayon and make a manhole rubbing to take home as a souvenir.

Address *Turtle Medallion*: just near Caffe Fantastico, 965 Kings Road, Victoria, BC V8T 1W7; *Moon Medallion*: near the Caribbean Village Cafe, 2646 Quadra Street, Victoria, BC V8T 4E4; *Molly's Original Cake Shop*: steps away from the Roxy Theatre, 2657 Quadra Street, Victoria, BC V8T 4E3, www.crd.bc.ca/landmarks/artworks | Getting there Varies by location | Hours Unrestricted | Tip Stop at locally owned and family-run Caffe Fantastico for a fantastic cappuccino and authentic Quadra Village vibes (965 Kings Road, www.caffefantastico.com).

6   Assassin's Corner

End of the road for Chong Wong

It's hard to imagine the tragedy that ended on this street corner over a century ago, but it was here that Chong Wong chose to put a gun to his head rather than face the law. Until just minutes before he pulled his trigger, the 35-year-old Wong was simply a local barber. But he was also a dedicated member of the Chinese Nationalist Party (or Kuomintang) based in southern China, which was led by Sun Yat-sen. So, when Wong read in the September 1, 1918 edition of the local Chinese newspaper that one of the Kuomintang's adversaries, Tang Hua Lung, was in town raising money for the new Chinese Republic, he decided to act. Tang wasn't just a political opponent to Chong – he was considered one of the founders of the new Chinese republican government and had served in the House of Representatives as speaker as well as minister of education and minister of the interior. He was also a prime target for assassination.

Chong traded his comb and scissors for a pair of revolvers and intercepted Tang as he was walking to an appointment at the Chinese Club at 555 Fisgard Street. What happened next was like a scene out of the Wild West. Chong pulled out both pistols and began shooting. He dropped Tang to the ground and killed him with a shot to the mouth. He then took a shot at a student visiting from Seattle, who dived to the pavement for cover. Then he took a shot at Tang's secretary Fei Lin, who ducked into a doorway. Then he chased the Chinese Consul Lingoh Wang down Government Street, firing indiscriminately at this point, narrowly missing the children and others scattering left and right as he ran east down Pandora Avenue. Wong got as far as Broad Street before bumping into Victoria's deputy fire chief. With the startled chief ahead and a crowd following behind, Wong raised a still-smoking gun one final time and put his final bullet in his own head.

Address Pandora Avenue & Broad Street, Victoria, BC V8W 0C6 | Getting there Bus 4, 11, 21, 22, 30, 31, 32, 47, 48, 53, 61, 65, 70, 71, 72, 75, 95 to Douglas & Pandora at City Hall | Hours Unrestricted | Tip Just a few steps north of this location you will find Spirit Square, a gateway of sorts to Centennial Square. Look for the *Two Brothers* cedar Spirit Poles by Butch Dick in the style of traditional Coast Salish house posts (622 Pandora Avenue, www.crd.bc.ca/landmarks/artworks/Two-Brothers--Spirit-Poles).

7 Baggins Shoes

Converse capital

Victoria may be the capital of British Columbia, and when it comes to Converse sneakers, the capital is right here on Johnson Street. Baggins Shoes has every type of Converse kicks you can possibly imagine. They have some 60,000 pairs in their inventory.

The shop's history dates back to the hippy days of 1969, and its initial offerings to customers were black-lights and black-light posters. If you're old enough, you'll know what those are. If you aren't then just know that they were far out and groovy. Another thing that was big then – and still big now – was JRR Tolkien's book *The Hobbit*, whose main character is one Bilbo Baggins. The name stuck.

The shop continued to evolve. By the 1990s, it began to develop a reputation as "the" place for Converse shoes. But the real showstopper, the thing that'll make you stop in your tracks, is the custom design and printing service. At Baggins, Converse shoes aren't just canvas – they are canvas for art!

It's actually kind of a big deal. They were known as the Duke and Duchess of Cambridge at the time, but when Prince William and Princess Kate visited Victoria in 2016, they were each presented with a pair of Converse Chuck Taylors with a custom Baggins design on them. Hollywood royalty also appreciate the ability to upgrade their sneakers with unique designs. Goldie Hawn has a pair, *Stranger Things* star Bobby Brown has a pair, and Yoko Ono has a pair with the words "love," "believe," and "imagine" on them. People from all walks of life love these arty wonders.

Bilbo Baggins warned his nephew Frodo that leaving home could be dangerous, saying "You step onto the road, and if you don't keep your feet, there's no knowing where you might be swept off to." But if you're looking for a new pair of Converse – or Vans or Doc Martens – this is where you might find something precious.

Address 580 Johnson Street, Victoria, BC V8W 1M3, +1 (250) 388-7022, www.bagginsshoes.com | Getting there Bus 10, 24, 25 to Johnson at Wharf | Hours Mon–Sat 10am–6pm, Sun 11am–5pm | Tip At the end of your shopping day, walk over to family-owned Il Terrazzo Restaurant for North Italian cuisine with a Pacific Northwest twist (535 Johnson Street, www.ilterrazzo.com).

8 The Bard & Banker Pub

Bucks, books, beer

For over a hundred years, this handsome pub at the corner of Government and Fort Streets was not a pub at all. It was a big, fancy bank. It started in 1888 as The Bank of British Columbia and was ground zero for newcomers keen to build the commercial and physical infrastructure of the region. Through these doors passed tradesmen, shopkeepers, real estate investors, prospectors, lumber merchants, miners, visionaries, gentlemen, scallywags, and also the occasional poet. The most famous poet was Robert W. Service, author of the epic Canadian works, *The Shooting of Dan McGrew* and *The Cremation of Sam McGee*.

Service worked here as a clerk around 1903, by which time the Bank of British Columbia had merged with the Canadian Bank of Commerce, and for a time he lived upstairs. He had learned the ropes in Scotland, but at age 21, like many other young men of his age and inclinations, he ditched the old country and came West seeking adventure. He odd-jobbed as a banker, ranch hand, and shop clerk up and down the West Coast. He eventually made it up to the Yukon, where his literary talents and all his life experiences coalesced into the timeless works that made him a household name along the same lines as Kipling and Twain.

While Service went on to literary fame, this building continued serving the citizens of Victoria right up until 1988. After 20 years as home to a retail business, the building, whose vaults once contained prospectors' gold, re-emerged as The Bard & Banker and started to pour golden pints of beer. Step through the substantial doorway, designed by the same architect who designed Craigdarroch Castle, and you'll immediately feel a bit richer. Pause to enjoy the Victorian opulence then raise a glass to the adventure-seekers, poets, writers, and others who drew their paychecks and their inspiration from here ages ago.

Address 1022 Government Street, Victoria, BC V8W 1Y3, +1 (250) 953-9993, www.bardandbanker.com | Getting there Bus 14, 15 to Fort at Wharf | Hours See website | Tip Across the street, look for the Southgate and Lascelles Building, built in 1869 on land that had previously been part of Fort Victoria. This is one of the earliest commercial buildings in the city; the second floor was added in 1887 (1102 Government Street).

9 — The Bay Street Armoury

Home to the Canadian Scottish Regiment's Museum

Ever since 1915, the Bay Street Armoury has been a dominant and historic feature of Victoria. Everyone knows it is headquarters to The Canadian Scottish Regiment. It is also home to one of the best regimental museums in Canada.

Here you'll see items from the earliest days of the Regiment, from its origins in 1913 to its participation in United Nations peacekeeping and NATO operations, to more recent action in Afghanistan. The museum also has a unique collection of Commonwealth cap badges, an impressive medal collection, and one of the most unique rifle collections in Canada. If you're lucky, you'll also see Canada's most-famous bagpipes (on loan from the Legislature): the legendary World War I pipes of James Richardson, VC.

Aside from the impressive military history and artefacts inside the Regimental Museum, the building itself is well worth a gander, even if just from the outside. Designated a National Historic Site in 1989, the building is a top-notch exemplar of the type of armouries and drill halls that were built across Canada in the early part of the twentieth century. Over a hundred like this were constructed from 1896 to 1918 and served as recruitment and training centres for almost every one of the 650,000 Canadians who served in World War I.

Like many other structures built for this purpose, the majestic, mighty, massive monstrosity is centred on a large two-story drill hall surrounded by armouries, storerooms, lecture rooms, and mess rooms. Architectural connoisseurs generally admire the building for its Tudor Revival style and draw attention to its central octagonal tower, with its crenelated parapet. The ceremonial balcony and its keystones combine to create an image of mediaeval fortifications. All of that rather makes the armoury sound like a fine wine. Or, given its high Scottish content, maybe a very fine single malt whisky.

Address 715 Bay Street, Victoria, BC V8T 1R1, +1 (250) 896-6938, www.canadianscottishregiment.ca | **Getting there** Bus 10 to Bay at Douglas at Westbourne | **Hours** Sep–May Tue 9am–2pm; Jun–Aug Tue–Fri 10am–3pm | **Tip** The staff member who lived on the second floor, above the safe, at the former Canadian Bank of Commerce building nearby was not as well armed as the soldiers – he was only issued with a pistol to ward off potential heisters (2420 Douglas Street).

10 The BC Aviation Museum
Lassie, a Lancaster, and a Lockheed

The quirky little secrets in a museum often make your visit more satisfying. At the BC Aviation Museum, you would expect to see some of the important historical aircraft that flew over the skies of BC. It's a given that there will be planes over 100 years old here, along with newer military aircraft, helicopters, seaplanes, and an array of other flying contraptions. But what does this small but really cool little museum have to do with the famous movie star dog Lassie?

To answer this perplexing bit of K9 aviation motion picture trivia, you need to go back to the 1930s, when the threat of World War II was looming. Around that time, the Canadian Government chose the present site of the Victoria International Airport as a military airfield. A decade later, in 1944, the Hollywood producers of the movie *Son of Lassie* chose that remote Royal Canadian Air Force base to shoot some scenes on location. It was a big production, starring Peter Lawford and June Lockhart from *Lost in Space* fame. Lancaster played an Air Force pilot, who, along with his dedicated dog Lassie, gets shot down behind enemy territory. (Spoiler alert: Lassie saves the day at the end of the movie.) The BC Aviation Museum has a picture in its Memorial Room of Lawford, along with the ever faithful Lassie, posing with members of RCAF 122 Squadron.

Most people don't come here to see a picture of a dog. A disassembled big warplane, the Avro Lancaster FM104, coincidentally built in Toronto the same year *Son of Lassie* came out, is a must see. Don't miss the Avro Anson MK IV and the E2 Sea Rover (the only example left in the world of this unique floatplane). The Lockheed T-33 Silver Star was the United States' first turbo-jet-powered combat plane and saw a lot of action in the Korean War before it was retired in 2002. That's the same year that the movie *Lassie, Best Friends are Forever* was released on DVD.

Address 1910 Norseman Road, North Saanich, BC V8L 5V5, +1 (250) 655-3300, www.bcam.net, info@bcam.net | Getting there Bus 71, 82, 87, 88 to Canora at Northbrook | Hours See website for seasonal hours | Tip Across the street is airplane-themed Mary's Bleue Moon Café, with hundreds of black and white photos, scale model planes, and good food (9535 Canora Road, Sidney, www.marysbleuemoon.com).

11 Beehive Wool Shop

Fibres from heaven

Founded in 1906 as Beehive Yarns and Dry Goods by the Fowler family, the Beehive started its life retailing yarn, fabric, and woollen underwear – very popular with the prospectors! The business has changed locations a few times in the last century and changed ownership too: the Orne family ran it for the last half of the last century until Valerie Huggett took over in 1997. Her daughter Julia joined her in 2018. Much has changed in the last century – they stopped selling dry goods decades ago. But, even if the families have changed over the years, this Victoria business icon is still a family-owned business, and it still has that "close knit" family feel to it.

As you enter the Beehive, your eyes will immediately be drawn up by the shop's high ceilings and then bedazzled by the rainbow of yarns displayed along the walls and on the racks. Yarns of every colour, brand, weight, and type abound: wool, cotton, cashmere, yak, silk, mohair, bamboo, angora, alpaca, and cotton, many made in Canada. They even have a curated section of hand-dyed yarns.

You can also find finished goods ready to wear – blankets, mittens, toques, and more, as well as books and kits to help you make your own woolly treasures. You'll find needle felting materials, knitting needles, stitch markers, darning eggs, moth repellent spray, and everything else you might possibly need either to get your knitting started or to fuel your established knitting passions. If you're looking for instruction, they can help with that too. They offer a number of in-person classes at the shop for all levels, from knitting newbies to seasoned pros. This place is a hive of knitting activity and darn worth visiting.

While the main sign for the shop is at the corner of Douglas and Fisgard Streets underneath the dramatic arched stone doorway of this century-old building, the actual entrance is a few steps away on Douglas Street.

Address 1700 Douglas Street, Victoria, BC V8W 2G7, +1 (250) 385-2727, www.beehivewoolshop.com | Getting there Bus 4, 11, 21, 22, 30, 31, 32, 47, 48, 53, 61, 65, 70, 71, 72, 75 to Douglas at Herald/Fisgard | Hours Mon–Sat 10am–5pm | Tip The Victoria Masonic Temple just around the corner was established in 1859 and is the oldest Masonic Lodge in British Columbia (650 Fisgard Street).

12 The Belfry Theatre

Puttin' on The Ritz

What would the Baptists who built this sanctified church in 1887 say if they knew that one day it would become the modern-day Belfry Theatre? Likely, "Bravo!"

Make no mistake about it: the Belfry is still a church with a big steeple to prove it, and its traditional inspiring architecture alone is worth the visit. The present-day, non-secular building oozes character, charm, intimacy, and, above all, authenticity. The Baptists constructed it originally at a cost of $8,000, with the intention of using it as a house of worship, which they did until 1971, when its congregation moved to Saanich. That's when the building became a shelter for the homeless, run by the Victoria Cool Aid Society. Extensive renovations have taken place through the years, and the first play that was staged in its present incarnation as a theatre was *Puttin' on the Ritz* in 1974.

This Victoria playhouse has been extremely busy. Since *Puttin' on the Ritz* was staged, the Belfry has produced over 330 plays. 238 of them have been Canadian productions, and 50 have been premiers. The 279-seat "little church-that-could" has built a worldwide reputation, and many of those premiere productions have gone on to gain international acclaim in the US, Australia, Europe, and London's West End. They continue to put on about 12 plays per year, and there is not a bad pew – or seat – in the house. The volunteers who run the Belfry Theatre are at the heart of its success. Like the Baptists who built it, they are hard-working and dedicated, and they believe in what they do. There are approximately 250 volunteers, including a few who have been there since the theatre's inception.

The founders of this Baptist Church 135 years ago would hopefully approve of the Belfry's present-day mission to produce theatre that generates ideas and dialogue, and that makes people see the world a little differently.

Address 1291 Gladstone Avenue, Victoria, BC V8T 1G5, +1 (250) 385-6815, www.belfry.bc.ca, boxoffice@belfry.bc.ca | Getting there Bus 22 to Fernwood at Grant | Hours See website for performance and events schedule | Tip On the plaza facing the Belfry is the Vegas Convenience Store, selling snacks and drinks and a good selection of handy household items. It's called Vegas Convenience because the boss who runs it has always wanted to go to Las Vegas one day (1284 Gladstone Avenue, Unit F).

13 Belleville Buskers

Pay to play

A busker is a person who performs music or other entertainment in the street for monetary donations. Victoria is full of them. It may be the temperate climate, the compact and tourist-dense nature of the Inner Harbour, the acoustically friendly outdoor building entrances and foyers, or the lively Victoria arts scene that attracts them from all around the world. They busk year-round, but it's in the summer that this old, colourful form of entertainment reaches a fevered pitch – in perfect pitch. Busking is such a big deal in Victoria that every year at the end of August, the city even stages the five-day Victoria Buskers Festival. The festival is a great way to witness mind blowing stunts, great music, dancing, comedy, and many other whacky forms of street entertainment.

But if you are not in Victoria for this annual, circus-like event, where is the best place to spot Buskers plying their trade for cash donations? Although buskers are nomadic by nature and move around a lot, Belleville Street, by the lower walkway of the Inner Harbour, is usually a good place to find them. It offers a high probability that you'll spot someone strumming a guitar and singing, or someone else juggling bowling balls and dishes while riding a unicycle blindfolded. The spots down there are coveted and even regulated. The city auditions buskers, assigns them exact spots, and gives them a schedule. The rest of the city is pretty much still a free for all.

In most cases, when it comes to busking, happy and engaged audiences are generous audiences. In recent years a few buskers have introduced modern commerce payment methods into their occupation, as some of them have touch tap terminals. Bring cash, bring your charge card, and remember that these people are trying to make a living through this joyous unique service. Above all just enjoy the energy and great entertainment!

Address Government & Belleville Streets, Victoria, BC V8V 1W9 | **Getting there** Bus 32, 47, 48, 53, 61, 65, 70, 71, 72, 95 to Legislative Terminal, then walk to the lower waterfront promenade directly in front of the Empress Hotel | **Hours** Unrestricted | **Tip** Behind the Inner Harbour, you'll find Canada's largest carillon. This white, 90-foot-tall bell tower was a gift to Canada from the Netherlands in 1967, and it chimes out musical notes from its 62 bells every hour (675 Belleville Street, www.royalbcmuseum.bc.ca).

14 Big Bad John's
Bring your big bad bra

Most of the bars and late-night dives from the early 1960s in Victoria are either gone or have morphed into something else. But time seems to have stood still at one notoriously weird and wild BC bar appropriately called Big Bad John's.

To understand the story behind this bar, a short history lesson on prohibition in the 1940s and early 1950s in BC is required. During that time, the Olsen family of Victoria fought hard to reverse some of the old-fashioned laws around the consumption of alcohol. In 1952, a plebiscite was held and passed by a very slim margin of just 1.5 percent, finally allowing booze to be sold by the glass in BC. All that hard work and lobbying by the Olsens had paid off, resulting in John Olsen opening BC's first ever cocktail bar, The Strathcona Lounge.

The bar had an auspicious opening on Canada Day in 1954, when, at 4 pm on July 1, they served the province's first-ever legal martini. Although the bar only seated 32 guests, the event was very exciting. Eight years later, the excitement continued with the World's Fair coming to nearby Seattle in 1962. To celebrate and cash in on all the American tourists passing through the region, the Strathcona Lounge changed its name to Big Bad John's Hillbilly Bar. It was meant to be a temporary promotional name and décor rebrand, but it has lasted for over 63 years.

Today, you will still find the walls at Big Bad John's covered from floor to ceiling with thousands of mementos that patrons have thumb-tacked up over the years, including a wild collage of IDs, money, business cards, and photos. Peanut shells cover the floor, and, in a real flashback to simpler times, bras and panties still hang from the rafters. What the bar's burlap-sack-upholstered benches lack in fashion, they make up for in function. Drop in and raise your glass in a toast to the bar's founder and namesake, the late John Olsen.

Address 919 Douglas Street, Victoria, BC V8W 2C2, +1 (250) 383-7137, https://strathconahotel.com/big-bad-johns | Getting there Bus 2, 3, 5, 10, 30, 31, 32, 47, 48, 53, 61, 65, 70, 71, 72, 75, 95 to Douglas at Courtney | Hours Daily 11:30–2am | Tip The roof of the Strathcona Hotel, right next door, has been converted into an outdoor beach volleyball court (919 Douglas Street, www.strathconahotel.com).

15 Bike Counters

Calculating the city's cycling citizens

An old axiom states, anything worth doing is worth measuring. By 2030, Victoria's goal is that 55 percent of all the trips within the city will be done by walking, cycling, or rolling. Right now, the number stands at 27 percent, which is the highest in Canada. Redfin, the US-based realty firm, ranked Victoria as the number one cycling city in Canada. So, if anyone asks, just tell them that Victoria is an extremely bike friendly city, and you'll have the empirical data to back it up. But where does that raw data come from?

Some of the numbers come from a network of electronic bike counters located around the city. It's a unique and very accurate way to track just how many people are cycling every day, and where they are cycling to and from. The high-tech digital counters went up over four years ago, and over a dozen of them are scattered around the city. By comparing cycling numbers year upon year and analysing trends, city planners can continue to improve what is already a great network of trails, bike paths, bike lanes, mixed-use pathways, and bike parking spots in Victoria.

Look for the counter on the Galloping Goose just south of the Bay Street Bridge in Vic West. It clocked nearly 800,000 cyclists pedalling past it in one year. That's an impressive average of over 2,000 bikes cruising by it each day. In the warmer months it averages 3,000 per day and has even gone as high as 4,000 cyclists a day travelling by. There are cyclists that pass the counters on their daily bike commutes and carefully track and record the numbers. It's fun to park your bike nearby and observe the electronic display slowly climb, knowing that your pedalling has boosted the count.

One of the most important features that makes cycling so desirable and easy in Victoria has very little to do with the urban planners. It's simply the fact that the city's terrain is fairly flat.

Address 383 Harbour Road, Victoria, BC V9A 3S1, www.crd.bc.ca/about/data/bike-counts |
Getting there Bus 10, 14, 15, 24, 25 to Esquimalt at Harbour | Hours Unrestricted |
Tip Recyclistas, a very colourful and offbeat full-service bike repair shop, recycling
depot, and educational workspace, is "the hub of Victoria's grassroots cycling community"
(25 Crease Avenue, www.recyclistas.ca).

16 — The Black Ball Line

200 years under the same flag

A company called The Black Ball Line operates a ferry service between Victoria and Port Angeles, Washington, 35 kilometres (22 miles) across the Strait of Juan de Fuca. They've been doing it for over 60 years, and pretty much everyone in Victoria knows the name of the old reliable ferryboat: the MV *Coho*, named after the silver salmon found in the waters of BC and Washington State. Ask someone where the name Blackball Lines comes from though, and you are likely to get a blank stare.

You must go back over 200 years for that answer. In 1818, Captain Charles H. Marshall founded the Black Ball Line. It was the first scheduled transatlantic service, sailing a fleet of clippers from Liverpool to New York. Graphics and logos were in their infancy back then, and they designed a simple yet enduring and easily recognizable flag to fly above the ships, featuring a black ball with a stark red background. In 1894, Marshall's grandson moved to Washington State, bringing the Blackball flag with him and establishing the Alaska Steamship Company, which grew to a fleet of five transport vessels and a destroyer escort.

Prior to the original Black Ball Line, Atlantic crossings were sporadic. The new service offered regular sailings from New York to Liverpool on the 5th day every month, and another ship sailing in the other direction on the first day of the month. You won't have to wait a month to jump onboard the *Coho* though. The 104-metre (341-foot) ship that carries up to 1,000 passengers offers two to four departures a day, depending on the time of the year. Since it began sailing in 1959, the *Coho* has carried over 26 million passengers.

As the ship sets sail, listen for an old, nostalgic, traditional theme song that will be played. The deep crooning voice you'll hear accompanying the whistles and the bells is none other than Bing Crosby, who grew up in Washington State.

Address 430 Belleville Street, Victoria, BC V8V 1W9, +1 (250) 386-2202, www.cohoferry.com |
Getting there Bus 30, 31, 75 to Legislature Terminal at Bellville Street | Hours See website for
seasonal schedule | Tip The old Steamship Building next door is a historic landmark in itself
that houses the aptly named Steamship Grill and Bar. Try the poke bowl (470 Belleville Street,
www.steamshipgrill.com).

17 Board with Friends Cafe
Get your game on

There's nothing like a clever double entendre to spark interest in a café's name. Yes, the word "board" has two totally different meanings. It's the one that refers to *Monopoly* and *Dungeons and Dragons* for which this place is famous. Nick Switzer, the co-owner of this hip and successful board game hang-out and café on Johnston Street, describes himself as the ultimate board game nerd while growing up. He was a carpenter for 14 years before deciding to pursue his real passion of board games and open this unique fun facility. You could say that he really made his dream come true.

Today, together with his partner Alyssa Chow, they have created a cool place with a friendly vibe and relaxed competitive board game culture, mixed with a real sense of community. They are all about remembering your name and your favourite game. They may even give you some tips on game strategy.

And it's a great spot for a bite to eat. Alyssa is the food lover, and as any committed board gamer knows, you can build up quite an appetite rolling the dice in *Risk* or while *Terraforming Mars*. The menu at Board with Friends consists of many flavours of milkshakes and smoothies, a variety of interesting panini sandwiches, and a good selection of cookies and pretzel snacks. The ever-popular board game staple – popcorn – is of course available in never-ending and abundant quantities. It almost goes without saying they offer coffee too.

Their "Stay and Play" policy means that you can pay $5.00 and just sit there all day playing games. And with over 600 games on file, it's a good thing that there is no time limit. If you want to drop in with your own games, no problem. Also, for people interested in purchasing board games, they carry Victoria's largest selection. People you don't know become friends at Board with Friends, and, despite the name, no one here seems bored.

Address 705 Johnson Street, Victoria, BC V8W 1M8, +1 (250) 590-6330, www.boardwithfriends.ca, info@boardwithfriends.ca | Getting there Bus 1, 2, 4, 24, 25 to Johnson at Douglas | Hours Mon–Thu 4–10pm, Fri 4pm–midnight, Sat 11am–midnight, Sun 11am–10pm | Tip The Haunted Manor Mini-Golf&Ping Pong Lounge, less than a block away, is a dark and scary "immersive twist" on a 15-hole mini-golf course (711 Yates Street, www.hauntedmanorvictoria.com).

18 BoulderHouse

Rock it to me!

If you're feeling cooped up, or if the weather is just not nice enough to tempt you into some outdoor activities, bouldering may be just the thing you need to get out of the house. BoulderHouse is the place to stretch your legs, arms, and mind.

For beginners used to being close to the ground, you'll be relieved to learn this is the kind of climbing that does not require ropes and a harness. Going way up high is not the point. Bouldering at BoulderHouse involves ascending a 13-foot-high wall with a bunch of colour-coded hand placements on a variety of fake rocks. Below is a very cushy mat that you can jump, drop, or fall onto at any time. The eight climbing circuits each include five or six 'problems' that you are challenged to overcome. It's not just about climbing – it's also about finding solutions. So, as you go through the circuits, you'll develop both physical strength and mental agility. And to keep things fresh, the experienced staff mixes up and resets the circuits weekly, so you'll never get bored.

BoulderHouse is Victoria's first bouldering-only climbing facility, opened in 2016, and is the brainchild of veteran climbers Jean-Marc de la Plante and Rob Somogyi. Jean-Marc has over 20 years of experience in the bouldering business, stretching all the way back to the "Allez-Up" recreation centre in Montreal, and has been bending over backwards to make climbing popular across the country. He places a special focus on making the sport accessible to people in urban locations with access to public transit. Rob has also been hanging around rocks for 20 years. Although he studied electrical engineering at UVic, it's the bouldering that gets him truly wired. Five years after starting BoulderHouse at this Victoria destination they partnered with the nearby City of Langford to open a brand new $3M facility complete with a dedicated kids' wall.

Address 2829 Quesnel Street, Victoria, BC V8T 4K2, +1 (778) 265-9342, www.boulderhouse.ca, climb@boulderhouse.ca | Getting there Bus 4, 9 to Hillside at Douglas | Hours Mon, Thu & Fri 9am–11pm, Tue 4–11pm, Wed 8am–11pm, Sat & Sun 9am–9pm | Tip A short walk away is Centennial Methodist Church (now Centennial United Church), established in 1985 and one of Victoria's oldest and most architecturally impressive churches (612 David Street, www.cucvictoria.com).

19 Bridge Disaster Plaque
Canada's worst streetcar disaster

In 1887, Victoria was the first city in Canada to be illuminated by an incandescent electric light station. By 1890, it had the first streetcar system in British Columbia and the third in Canada. Residents were proud that their community on the West Coast of the newly confederated country was quickly becoming among its most urban and modern. But the warm embrace of progress suffered a chilling reversal on May 26, 1896, when 55 citizens lost their lives in a horrific tragedy known as The Point Ellice Bridge Disaster.

The day was supposed to be one of celebration. Queen Victoria had just become the longest-reigning monarch in British history, and her subjects were keen to express their loyalty and pride. Citizens had planned a "birthday carnival," including a mock naval battle at Esquimalt, a few kilometres from downtown. To get there, one could walk, ride a horse, take a horse-drawn carriage, or take the electric streetcar over Point Ellice Bridge. According to *The Daily Colonist*, streetcar number 16 "was hurrying to the scene of the sham battle, freighted to its capacity and beyond with holiday-makers, when in an instant mirth was turned into mourning and between 50 and 60 souls were hurried into eternity."

Two horse-drawn carriages also followed the car into the water, as did a bicyclist who was struck by a piece of metal that shattered his skull. *The Daily Colonist* further stated, "The hour was not without its heroes who were quick to think and act, and to these heroes, women and men, the salvation of many lives from the waters is due, as well as the winning back from death of many who had all appearances passed into the shadowland." Nearly 100 survived, but for many years afterwards, the annual birthday celebrations would be mixed with unforgettable sorrow for those who were lost. All that remains now are distant memories – and this plaque.

POINT ELLICE BRIDGE DISASTER

AT 1:50 PM ON 26 MAY 1896 AN OVERLOADED STREETCAR PLUNGED THROUGH THE ROTTEN DECK OF THE OLD POINT ELLICE BRIDGE. FIFTY FIVE PEOPLE WERE KILLED IN WHAT HAS BECOME NORTH AMERICA'S WORST STREETCAR ACCIDENT.

Address 265–321 Bay Street, Victoria, BC V8T 1S6, on the east side of the Point Ellice Bridge, north side of the street | Getting there Bus 10 to Bay at Turner, or bus 14 to Tyee at Bay. The plaque is hidden in the grass on your right. | Hours Unrestricted | Tip The steam plant that generated the electrical power for the original streetcar system still stands within eyesight of the bridge disaster. The monolithic building is now home to a sustainable apparel company called "ecologyst" (2110 Store Street, www.ecologyst.com).

20 British Columbia Archives

The mini-Menzies portraits and millions more

There are a million things to find in the Archives of British Columbia – much more than a million in fact. The institution actually safeguards more than 5,000,000 photographs; 180,000 maps, plans, and architectural records; 90,000 boxes of government records; and some 10,300 paintings, drawings, and prints. Some are items you'd expect; others are rather surprising. The oldest archives west of the Great Lakes, the Archives joined the Royal BC Museum in 2003.

Among the most unusual items are the palm-sized, miniature portraits of Scottish doctor and botanist Archibald Menzies (1754–1842) and his wife Janet (1770–1837). The two portraits were created by artist Thomas Richmond at his London studio in 1802, the same year the couple married. The gold-framed watercolour of Archibald is painted on a sheet of ivory and shows him at age 48, wearing a blue velvet frock coat. On the reverse is a glass pane showing locks of Archibald's hair, braided and thatched. Janet's portrait is in a wooden frame, painted red like *The Red Violin* and giving off the same intriguing vibe.

Most people know Archibald sailed around Vancouver Island with Captain Vancouver on HMS *Discovery* from 1791 to 1795. Fewer know he first set foot here in 1787 at Nootka Sound with James Colnett aboard the fur trading ship *The Prince of Wales* and was among the first Europeans to befriend Chief Maquinna. The Archives have strict rules about reproducing photographs of their collections, so if you want to see these miniatures, you'll have to make an appointment to go see them in person. It's more rewarding to go and see precious artefacts in real life anyway.

In addition to these mini marvels and mysteries, you'll find much of British Columbia's most precious historical treasures at the Archives. Get started by searching the 1,000,000 digital images on the Archives' website.

Address BC Archives, 655 Bellevue Street, Victoria, BC V8W 1A1, +1 (250) 356-7226, www.royalbcmuseum.bc.ca/archives/visit, receptionist@royalbcmuseum.bc.ca | Getting there Bus 30, 31, 75 to Legislature Terminal | Hours By appointment only, unrestricted from outside | Tip Around the corner from the Archives, you'll find the headquarters of the Victoria Historical Society (234 Menzies Street, www.victoriahistoricalsociety.bc.ca).

21 Butchart Gardens

From rocks to roses

Everyone loves a garden, but there's something extra special about a garden that grows on a reclaimed industrial site. It's hard to believe it when you look at it today, but Butchart Gardens was once a big, open, barren, empty, rock quarry. It got that way thanks to cement pioneer Robert Butchart.

Butchart arrived in Victoria in 1902 and immediately got to work turning limestone into bags of cement, quenching the thirst of architects, builders, and various industrialists sprouting up all along the fast-growing port cities of Victoria, Seattle, and San Francisco. For three years, Butchart's workers swung their pickaxes, crushed rock, and pummelled the ground until all that was left was a huge hole in the ground. The workers moved on to other work sites, but poor Jennie Butchart, Robert's wife, was not happy about the mess. So, she decided to turn it into a garden.

For the next 15 years, she moved topsoil into the pit, re-formed rubble into strategically placed landscape features, arranged ivy in the bald quarry walls, and built a miracle. She also built a reputation. Word got around. People had to come and see for themselves just what she was doing. It started with friends and neighbours coming over for a looky-loo, but soon the gardens were attracting complete strangers – thousands of them. Keep in mind this was still just a private home garden, not a business or a tourist attraction. And Jennie even served her guests a cup of tea. It's no wonder she was named Victoria's Best Citizen in 1930.

The garden has seen many changes since those early days, including the passing of Robert and Jennie. But unlike some ancient wonders, it's still here to be enjoyed today. These lush 55 acres, tended by almost as many gardeners, are waiting to please your senses with 900 bedding plant varieties and 26 greenhouses … and over 2,500 rose bushes.

Address 800 Benvenuto Avenue, Victoria, BC V8M 1J8, +1 (250) 652-4422, www.butchartgardens.com | Getting there Bus 75, 81 to Butchart Gardens | Hours See website for seasonal hours | Tip The land here is the traditional territory of the WSÁNÉC people, so look for the two Totem Poles created by Master Carvers Charles Elliot of the Tsartlip Nation and Doug La Fortune of Tsawout Band. They're in the centre of the Gardens, a short walk north from the Rose Carousel.

22 The Capital Iron Building
From flour makers to shipbreakers

One of Victoria's oldest and most famous shops was on a street called Store Street. The Capitol Iron building has been around since 1863, four years before confederation. For decades it housed the Capital Iron Store, a quintessential general store selling almost everything anyone might need, even irons, but that's not how the store got its name.

The building was originally a waterfront warehouse and office. Back in the 1860s, Canada was moving full steam ahead on building the national railway from coast to coast, and hungry Chinese labourers needed to be fed. Rice was shipped in from Asia and milled at the Victoria Roller and Flour Mill, which operated from the Store Street location until 1897, when they went bust and another rice mill moved in. Eventually, the Canadian government's heavy protectionist taxes on imported and unprocessed grain put that mill out of business as well. The building sat vacant for 17 years.

Then, in 1934, a commercial enterprise specialising in marine scrap metal took over. That's where the unusual name comes in. Since the owner Morris L. Green was in the business of salvaging iron and his operations were located in the province's capital, it made perfect sense to call the place Capital Iron & Metals. After World War II came to an end, many old Navy ships were scrapped, and business was good. At the same time the Government was selling off large amounts of military surplus items. Capital Iron became a reseller of old uniforms, boots, bags, and other military gear; hence the entry into retail sales, which eventually led to the general store that operated for 70 years.

The Capital Iron Store didn't survive the global pandemic and shut its doors at the end of 2022. The beautiful old building will soon be preserved and redeveloped to be part of an area including arts and cultural facilities, high-tech office space, and more retailers.

Address 1900 Store Street, Victoria, BC V8T 4R4 | **Getting there** Bus 14, 15, 24, 25 to Pandora at Courtney at Store | **Hours** Unrestricted from the outside | **Tip** Stop by Value Village Thrift Store just down the street, which resold many of the items originally from Capital Iron. This is the largest branch in BC and the second largest in Canada (1810 Store Street, www.stores.savers.com/bc/victoria/valuevillage-thrift-store-2010.html).

23 — Centennial Time Capsule

"The future for us is the past and present for you"

Mark this date on your calendar: January 1, 2067. That's when a bunch of elected officials, many of whom haven't even been born yet, will gather at the Confederation Court to open up a 100-year-old time capsule. The capsule's contents include exactly 100 items intended to be revealed to celebrate the 200th anniversary of Canada.

It's actually in an eight-foot-long, carefully sealed, plastic vacuum tube with a brass plaque on top to mark the spot. And since the tube is encased in a heavy-duty, rectangular, concrete box, some type of hydraulic hoist will have to be on hand to lift it.

It ought to be a momentous occasion when they finally crack it open. But since there is a good chance that your calendar for 2067 is starting to fill up, and it's likely that you won't be able to make it to the official unveiling, we will spill the beans and let you know its contents. Remember, the year that it was buried was 1967, and the entire country was giddy celebrating its 100th anniversary. People at the time wanted to put meaningful artefacts and items of historical and social significance into the capsule to give future British Columbians an idea of what that wonderful year of celebrations was like.

[Spoiler Alert] Here's what's inside: The words and music to the song *Can-A-Da*, written and performed at the time by that funny musician with the jewel-studded horn, Bobby Gimby. The song was a huge hit in 1967, blaring out of every transistor radio in Victoria at the time. The time capsule also contains Centennial medallions, folders, guides books, calendars, flags, fashion pictures, maple leaf pins and decals, programs of centennial year events, centennial place mats, and a series of historical sketches of BC Pioneers from the *Victoria Times* newspaper. William Bennet, the premiere at the time, even left this message, "The future for us, is the past and present for you."

Address Confederation Garden Court at Menzies & Belleville Streets, Victoria, BC V8V 1X3 | Getting there Bus 32, 53 to Legislature Terminal | Tip 1871 was the year that the province of British Columbia actually joined the confederation. In 1971, another time capsule was buried near the Bell Tower by the Provincial Museum, less than 500 metres from this one. If you miss the 2067 opening, this capsule will be opened in 2071 (675 Belleville Street, www.royalbcmuseum.bc.ca).

24 CFB Esquimalt Naval and Military Museum

This lady was no dummy

When Sheila Kidd was a young girl living in Victoria in the early 1940s, she developed throat ulcers that made it difficult to move her lips when she spoke. For years, to ease the pain, she learned to talk without moving her lips. She then parlayed those skills into becoming a professional ventriloquist, which was an unusual profession for a woman at the time.

When you visit the incredibly well-curated Naval Museum on the Esquimalt base, you will see a glass case containing an old ventriloquist's dummy named Spike Ryan, dressed in a white sailor suit and tucked away in a corner on the huge base. When Kidd joined the navy in 1943, she brought that red-headed, wooden prop with her. Her act was such a hit that the Navy immediately assigned her and Spike Ryan to perform in a popular touring show called "Meet the Navy."

Starring in the show was a demanding gig. Mornings and afternoons were spent rigorously rehearsing, and some days saw multiple shows. Part of her onstage schtick involved Kidd being invariably respectful to the officers in the show, while Spike was usually a bit disrespectful and salty. The promotional show toured towns across Canada and eventually played in the United Kingdom. Kidd was discharged from service on November 23, 1945 and continued working with her partner Spike until 1959. Not much is known about her after that.

But in 2011, Spike surfaced in a thrift shop in Alberta! He was stashed away in an old suitcase with some RCN snapshots and archival documents that were helpful in his return to the Esquimalt base.

There is so much more to see in the Museum so give yourself at least an hour or two to look around. The building that houses the museum was built in the 19th century with red bricks brought around Cape Horn in a sailboat.

Address Naden 5 CFB Esquimalt, Esquimalt, BC V9A 7N2, +1 (250) 363-5655, www.navalandmilitarymuseum.org | **Getting there** By car, take Government Street and then turn left on Wharf Street, over the Johnson Street Bridge, and then follow Esquimalt Road for 6 kilometres (3.73 miles) to Hospital Road, which leads you to the base. | **Hours** Daily 10am–3:30pm | **Tip** Nearby Saxe Point Park offers some spectacular views of the Olympic Mountains and the Strait of Juan de Fuca. During World War II, many of the trees had to be cleared when a searchlight was installed as part of the Department of National Defence's wartime initiatives (the south end of Fraser Street, Esquimalt, www.esquimalt.ca).

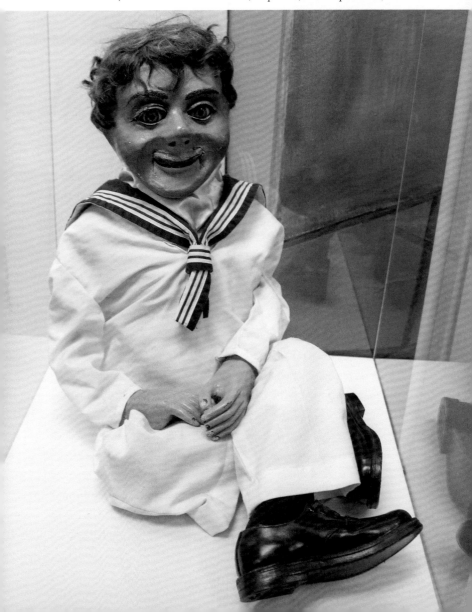

25 Charlie's Trail Hand-Cranked Audio

Voices from the past

As if following a furiously rushing stream through an amazingly verdant and plush coastal forest isn't enough, this mini adventure along Charlie's Trail will also take you past a small, picturesque waterfall. Near the end of the trail, something completely different awaits. When you spin the handle of this hand-cranked green machine, it offers eight different interpretative audio vignettes. The audio is clear, with interesting messages delivered by two noteworthy and respected narrators. Leave your earbuds at home.

Charlie's Trail is located on the grounds of Royal Roads University in the woods adjacent to the campus. It runs along Colwood Creek, following the winding waters downhill into Esquimalt Lagoon. The well-groomed trail and the university are located on the traditional lands of the Xwsepsum (Esquimalt) and Lkwungen (Songhees) Nations. While walking along, imagine how generations of these people hunted, fished, and gathered what they needed from what lies below your feet.

Near the bottom of Charlie's Trail, a hand-powered audio box offers up eight different pre-recorded soundtracks describing the plants and trees you just passed, and how they were used to make traditional tools, shelter, and vital medicines. It is important to note that the recordings are in two different languages by Esquimalt Chief Edward Thomas (Seenupin) who speaks in English, and by Songhees Nation Elder Elmer Seniemten George. George is the last fluent speaker of the Lekwungen language.

While you're surrounded by this wonderful theatre of nature, reflect on Elder George's voice, its resonance, his inflections and tonality, and his almost-forgotten language's significance. And all of these sights, sounds, and sensations are yours on a mere 30-minute walk.

Learn about the trees
and plants found on
this trail in Lkwungen
and English.

SELECT NUMBER / TURN UNTIL MESSAGE PLAYS

LISTEN & ENJOY!

Address On the grounds of Royal Roads University, 2005 Sooke Road, Victoria, BC V9B 5Y2, next to the intersection of University Drive and College Drive, www.colwood.ca/discover-colwood/parks-trails/royal-roads-forest | **Getting there** Bus 39, 48, 51, 52, 55, 61 to Sooke Road at Acacia | **Hours** Unrestricted | **Tip** To commemorate the 75th anniversary of Royal Roads University, a totem pole was erected just up the road from the hand-crank, honouring the Indigenous people and their ancestral land (at the intersection of University Drive and West Campus Road, www.royalroads.ca).

26 _ Chief Maquinna Statue
Iconic leader cast in stone

Not a lot of people know about Chief Maquinna, and even fewer people know there's an image of him among the British Columbia Legislature Buildings. At the east entrance of the Legislative Library, look up to your left to see him there gazing out toward the Pacific.

Maquinna, one of the most important figures in British Columbia's history, was chief of the Nuu-chah-nulth people and lived in the area of Vancouver Island known as Nootka Sound. It was there that he met Spanish Captain Juan Perez as he was passing by in 1774, and British Captain James Cook, who lingered on shore in 1778. Over the following years, Chief Maquinna was sought out by all the explorers interested in the possibilities of trans-Pacific trade, as they courted his friendship and allegiance. Trade ships from Canton, London, and Boston all charted courses for Nootka Sound and sought the friendship of the chief. As the gatekeeper to inland trade, Maquinna held great political power and influence. He could make things go smoothly or not, and over time he would do both.

Chief Maquinna's is one of fourteen statues on the exterior façade of the Legislative Library Building. The statue was carved by Charles Marega, who also carved the lions at Vancouver's Lion's Gate Bridge. The other thirteen statues are on the exterior of the library. Also look for six circular medallions featuring the images of prominent literary figures from European history: Homer, Dante, Shakespeare, Sophocles, Milton, and Socrates.

The roof of the Legislative Library includes four domes, and on the three outward-facing corners of each dome are three statues of female muses. Each of the twelve statues has four styles: Music, Sculpture, Painting, and Architecture. While the main BC Legislature Building was completed by 1897, the Legislative Library and these handsome statues were not finished until 1915.

Address East side of the Legislative Library of British Columbia, 501 Belleville Street, Victoria, BC V8V 1X4, www.leg.bc.ca/dyl/Pages/Chief-Maquinna.aspx | Getting there Bus 2, 3, 5 to Superior at Menzies | Hours Unrestricted | Tip The Speaker's Chair, a public sculpture located in the Speaker's Courtyard on the east side of the library, is the perfect place for a quasi-regal photo opportunity.

27 — The Chinese Public School
Icon of history and architecture

This strikingly impressive building, set back from the street and re-splendent in red-coloured lanterns, pagoda-style roofline, and bold red doors is one of the most remarkable buildings located in one of the oldest Chinatowns in North America.

Its origins are regrettable – it was built following a 1908 Victoria School Board policy that prevented Chinese-born children from at-tending public schools until they had learned to speak English. Yet it stands and remains an incredible and permanent testament to the Chinese Canadian community's strength and determination to over-come adversity and prosper. The two-story, ten-room building was commissioned by the Chinese Consolidated Benevolent Association, and, surprisingly, the architect they chose for the job was not Chinese but Scottish: 26-year-old David Cowper Frame, who got the gig for perhaps the greatest masterpiece of his career.

The building is considered by historians to be a special gem in the city partly because of its eclectic architectural elements, like the trefoil fretwork in the second-floor balcony, the orientalized bracketed eaves, and the first and second-floor window muntin pattern (the way the glass panes are separated by wood strips within the window frame). But there is no single element or set of features that make it so re-markable. Rather, it is the whole ensemble that makes it so impressive: the windows, the roof line, the tower, the stairs, the courtyard, the fence, the gate posts, and more – the whole package packs a punch.

Things have changed a lot since 1908, and foreign-born students from China and around the world are welcome in all of Victoria's public schools. Nevertheless, the Chinese Public School – still used for supplementary educational services to the Chinese community – stands as an important and beautiful reminder of past challenges and community strength.

Address 636 Fisgard Street, Victoria, BC V8W 1R6, +1 (250) 384-7352 | Getting there Bus 4, 11, 21, 22, 30, 31, 32, 47, 48, 53, 61, 65, 70, 71, 72, 75 to Douglas at Herald/Fisgard | Hours Unrestricted | Tip Walk back toward Government Street, and you'll find three colourful and impressive Chinatown Heritage Murals by artist Jeff Maltby (www.artsvictoria.ca/jeffmaltby).

28 __ Colwood Fire Museum
Don't miss the fire-engine-red bike

The excellent Colwood Fire Fighters Historical Museum that sits in a small building adjacent to the working firehall is strictly a volunteer operation. The passion demonstrated by the volunteers for both the station and the museum is clearly evident when you visit the complex on Metchosin Road.

The first thing that grabs your attention as you pull open the museum's front door and look up is an upside-down bouquet of a hundred old fire hoses dangling down from the ceiling. Take a few more steps inside, and you'll see a beautiful, shining artefact that can best be described as the heart of every firehall in the world: a fire truck. This big red one is a 1944 International K8. It started its long-storied service at the Victoria airport during World War II. It then began its tenure in Colwood in 1957 and extinguished a lot of flames there until it was pulled from active duty in 1977.

But like the hoses as you enter that are above your head, one of the most interesting finds in the museum is also hanging way up high near the ceiling. It is an old fire-engine-red bicycle with an interesting past as one of Colwood's very first emergency vehicles. The bike belongs to the fire hall's longest serving volunteer Alan Emery. His grandfather gave it to him during the war to assist him in getting to his volunteer job at the hall. The air-raid sirens at the time were meant to alert local residents of an emergency, and their high-pitched wailing sound was the que for a 15-year-old Emery to hop on that bike and pedal like crazy to answer the call. At the former hall, which was then on Sooke Road, a rickety old vegetable truck that had been hastily outfitted with a hose and pump awaited him. Emery still resides in Colwood, and his bike has long since been retired. If you hear an alarm sounding next door during your visit to the museum, you may find your tour delayed.

Address 3215 Metchosin Road, Victoria, BC V9C 2A4, +1 (250) 478-8321, www.colwood.ca |
Getting there Bus 48, 52, 54, 55, 59 to Metchosin at Wishart | **Hours** By appointment only |
Tip The Royal Bay Bakery is just down the road from the museum. They have great coffee and
pastries and sell the most delicious honey on Vancouver Island (3337 Metchosin Road,
www.royalbaybakery.com).

29 Congregation Emanu-El
The oldest synagogue on North America's West Coast

Jewish law states that a synagogue is a place where a minimum of 10 men can gather for worship and study. Victoria's Congregation Emanu-El, built in 1863, surpasses that criterion. It can also lay claim to being the oldest synagogue on the West Coast of North America, which is even more unusual when you compare the size of Victoria to Los Angeles, San Francisco, Portland, and Seattle. Incidentally, the first and oldest synagogue in Canada is the Shearith Israel Synagogue in Montreal, which has relocated three times but originally was built in 1768.

Congregation Emanu-El owns many other "firsts" when it comes to its prominent members who attended services here over the years. Lumley Franklin (1808–1873) was British North America's first Jewish mayor and the second mayor of Victoria. Henry Nathan Jr. (1842–1914), Canada's first Jewish representative elected to the House of Commons in 1882, worshipped here as well. Samuel Schultz (1865–1917) was the country's first Jewish judge.

The original Jewish settlers who built the synagogue arrived in Canada from the United States like so many others during the Fraser Canyon Gold Rush. Most of them came from San Francisco in 1858 with a huge wave of prospectors hoping to strike it rich. They all had to pass through the capital city of Victoria to purchase their mining licences before heading over to the mainland. The Jewish arrivals accompanied prospectors and supplied their camps and early settlements with food, clothing, tools, tents, and other household items. During the 1850s, there were about 200 Jewish people in Victoria. Towards the end of that century though Victoria's Jewish population continued to decline as the city of Vancouver took on more and more prominence. By the mid-1940s there were only 10 paid-up families in the synagogue's dwindling congregation. Today about 250 families attend services there.

Address 1461 Blanshard Street, Victoria, BC V8W 2J3, +1 (250) 382-0615, www.congregationemanuel.ca | Getting there Bus 2, 5, 27, 28 to Pandora at Blanshard | Hours See website for tours of the synagogue and services | Tip The Jewish Cemetery of Victoria was created in 1860 and continues to serve the Jewish community of Victoria, Vancouver Island, and the nearby Islands (2750 Cedar Hill Road, www.jewishcemeteryofvictoriabc.ca).

30__ Cook Street Food Truck Village

A moveable feast

Victoria has a thriving food truck trade. Altogether, about 50 of them serve up breakfast, lunch, and dinner 7 days a week, cooking up everything from chilli to Chinese to grilled cheese. Mounted on four wheels, insured, and licenced, these colourful, fully mobile trucks tend to move around a lot though. So, it's sometimes hard to pin down exactly where they are parked or will be moving to next. Sure, some apps such as streetfoodapp.com might be able help you find a food truck nearby to subdue your street hunger pangs.

But there is also one trusty and reliable place in Victoria where you will always find two or three of them parked and cooking something tasty behind their sliding window. Think of it as the local hang out for some of those peripatetic epicurean vans. The Cook Street Food Truck Village was established just before the pandemic broke out and managed to survive throughout its two-year grip. Plenty of outdoor seating, a washroom with an outdoor entrance, together with buckets of hand sanitizer and stacks of masks proved to be a winning formula during Covid 19. The small Food Truck Village actually did quite well while some restaurants on Cook Street, which is a real foodie area, were closed. The Village continues to thrive by offering great food, a cool vibe, plenty of fresh air, and a wide variety of selections that originate from separate menus.

There are plenty of enticing food trucks all over Victoria to look out for. Many of them have names that are hard to forget, like BeaverTails Mobile, Deadbeetz Burgers, Hard Hat Cafe, The Love Perogy, Sub Zero Ice Cream, Taco Justice, Uni-Corn Treats, Taste-Buds, and finally, one that belongs in the *111 Places Los Angeles* book, a food truck named Straight Outta Chompton.

Address 325 Cook Street, Victoria, BC V8V 3X5 | Getting there Bus 3, 7 to Cook at Sutlej |
Hours Daily 8am–2pm | Tip Get your meal to go and wander down a few blocks to Spiral
Beach to watch the dynamic and adventurous kite boarders manoeuvre their colourful large
kites propelling them over the choppy waves and boosting big air (Cook Street at Dallas Road).

31__The Costume Museum
Regal regalia at Cary Castle Mews

Earlier this century, someone was tidying up the attic of Government House and found a trove of fancy dresses. It turns out that each dress had been made for the wife of the serving lieutenant governor. Stunning in appearance, well-preserved, and each one a snapshot of high-society fashion for their respective era, they simply had to be put on display. You can see them at the Costume Museum. This collection of dresses is known as the Chatelaine Collection, as the word "chatelaine" indicates the woman who is head of an impressive household.

These and many other fascinating costumes associated with courtly life can be seen right up close; there are no stanchions or glass cases here to keep you at arm's length. The volunteers are absolute encyclopaedias of information and will fill you with knowledge and hospitality.

In addition to ladies' gowns, you'll also see a fine, horse-drawn carriage once used by Prince Andrew, and a handmade court tunic, complete with silver bullets, of the kind that would have been used by a Georgian prince. In another part of the museum are military costumes used when the lieutenant governor is representing the Crown at formal occasions. You'll see the style of dress worn by the Aide-de-Camp, members of the Royal Canadian Mounted Police, and at the formal, hand-made, bespoke military mess dress tunics worn by the lieutenant governor, including one with spectacular gold braided orca and eagle symbols made for Iona Campagnolo, British Columbia's first woman lieutenant governor.

The Costume Museum will stimulate fashion aficionados and historians alike. Known as the Cary Castle Mews, this little-known cluster of wooden service buildings were built in the 1870s and consisted of the stables, a carriage house, a jail, a root cellar, a wash house, and a poultry house, all of which used to support the operations of Government House.

Address Government House, 1401 Rockland Avenue, Victoria, BC V8S 1V9, www.ltgov.bc.ca/costume-museum | **Getting there** Bus 1 to Richardson at Kipling | **Hours** See website for seasonal hours | **Tip** Look for the original 1959 Hosaqami totem pole, located between the interpretive centre and the carriage house, as you head toward the tea house for a refreshment.

32   Craigflower School
Western Canada's oldest schoolhouse

Not only is this the oldest surviving public building in British Columbia, it is also the oldest schoolhouse in Western Canada. Built in 1854, Craigflower School is also among a handful of buildings erected before the Gold Rush of 1858, and it's actually older than Canada itself.

The school was built for the children of The Hudson's Bay Company's Craigflower Farm and the surrounding area. This farm was the senior of four farms on the island and named after the Craigflower Estate in Scotland, owned by Andrew Colville, the Governor of The Hudson's Bay Company. The farm provided food to Fort Vancouver, and its establishment marked the beginning of the area's transition from commercial fur trade to permanent settlement. In its early days, the nearby manor house was a centre of social life for Victoria residents and Royal Navy officers from Esquimalt.

The schoolhouse had a single schoolroom on the first floor and six rooms for the teacher Charles Clark, his family, and student boarders from other parts of Vancouver Island. Clark gave lessons in reading, writing, arithmetic, history, geography, grammar, geometry, and algebra – pretty much everything – to the twenty-one students, who ranged in age from four to sixteen. A large, brick fireplace and the cooking stove provided heating for the building. When the American steamship *Major Thompkins* was shipwrecked in 1854, her bell was salvaged and hung in the yard to call students to class. Initially, the school was accessible from the main part of the farm only by boat, but the 1856 completion of the first Craigflower bridge linked the two parts of the farm together.

Architecturally, the value of the schoolhouse lies in its utilitarian form and simple construction, which provide insight into the functional nature of the province's earliest public works. It and the manor are both National Historic Sites.

Address 2755 Admirals Road, Victoria, BC V9A 2R2 | Getting there Bus 24, 25 to Admirals at Gorge, or bus 14 to Craigflower at Admirals | Hours Unrestricted from the outside | Tip Iluka Espresso is easy to miss but great to find if you want to refresh yourself with a coffee, tea, snack, and views of Portage Inlet (101 Island Highway, Suite 100, www.ilukaespresso.ca).

33 Dancing Ferries
Water Ballet

The shortest distance between two points is a straight line. But sometimes, that's not the point at all. Looking out onto Victoria's Inner Harbour, you'll see several bright, 10-passenger water taxis travelling back and forth. They stand out because their colour and graphic design scheme is similar to New York's old Checker cabs – a yellow background with black and white squares. They are also referred to as harbour ferries, pickle boats, and, for four months of the year, they assume the moniker, "Dancing Ferries." These are ferries with a creative side.

Harbour Ferries launched a service in Victoria in 1990, and, as the name implies, their main purpose was to transport tourists and locals from point A to point B. Most of the Captains are retired men and women with the gift of the gab, who love telling stories about the unique and picturesque city. It didn't take long for these captains to discover that without passengers aboard, the boats became far more manoeuvrable. Taking one part inspiration from the world famous RCMP Musical Ride, and one part inspiration from synchronised swimming, a new tradition was born. Every summer, the Dancing Ferries stage scheduled free performances in the downtown inner harbour, where they twirl in beautifully timed sequences choreographed to music. The colourful boats pushed to their limits, they waltz on the waves, zigging and zagging and intertwining with one another, tripping the light fantastic on the ocean. It's fun to watch them from anywhere on the shore and there is nothing else quite like it.

When they are not dancing, they are working. They provide different sightseeing tours, even a pub crawl tour, and basic transportation between drop off points in the busy harbour every day of the year. Altogether, there are 18 boats in the fleet, and over 120 people now are employed by this innovative company.

Address Multiple landings, www.victoriaharbourferry.com, +1 (250) 514-9794 | Getting there Varies by location | Hours Daily 1am–4pm, check website for schedule based on weather conditions | Tip Prince of Whales is the most popular company in Victoria to offer whale watching tours (812 Wharf Street, www.princeofwhales.com).

34__David Foster's Childhood Home

Can you see St Elmo's Fire from here?

David Foster, he of over a dozen Grammy Awards and a contact list of Who's Who that includes all the members of the Who, started his life as a professional musician when he was just 16. But up until that time, the musical prodigy's formative years were spent at this bungalow, built by his father in 1949, a year before Foster was born. Still a private home, this three-bedroom house was typical of the era, and Foster lived here with his six older sisters – he had his own room in the basement. Take a moment to imagine a young David tinkling away on the piano they had in the living room.

This neighbourhood 5 kilometres (3 miles) from downtown Victoria might just as well have been a million miles away from the bright lights of New York, London, and Paris, but that didn't stop Foster from taking the ferry over to Vancouver in 1970 to form a band called Skylark. The next year, he went even further. As a Los Angeles session player, he picked up gigs with big names like John Lennon, George Harrison, Barbra Streisand, and Rod Stewart. As a producer, he worked with Alice Cooper, Boz Scaggs, and produced albums for Daryl Hall and John Oates. He wrote for Earth, Wind & Fire, and created hits for Chicago and Lionel Richie. He wrote the soundtrack for the 1985 movie *St. Elmo's Fire*.

Most Canadians know David best for writing the theme song for the 1988 Winter Olympic Games. High-profile collaborations include his work on Whitney Houston's *I Will Always Love You* and Céline Dion's *The Power of Love*. Over four decades, Foster has worked on just about everything and with just about everyone.

Despite all that international glamour and fame, David Foster still has a deep connection to Victoria. The heart of his affection remains this little bungalow on Ascot Drive.

Address 3915 Ascot Drive, Victoria, BC V8P 3S2 | Getting there Bus 17 to Cedar Hill Cross at Marjean | Hours Unrestricted from the outside only | Tip Close by is King's Pond, the place where all the most regal ducks hang out. If young David had not become a music mogul, he might easily have become an ornithologist (Queensbury Avenue at Ascot Drive).

35 The Dinosaur Lab

Wanna buy a slightly used dinosaur bone?

Now for something old and completely different. Dinosaur bones are typically displayed at public museums around the world. There are some impressive private collections as well. Most people have seen a fossil or two in their lifetime, and while observing these beautiful, massive, prehistoric creatures, the first questions that come to mind are usually how old it is, what it is, and where it lived. But you've probably never wondered where it was restored. The answer could be Victoria.

The Dinosaur Lab on Dupplin Road started out in 2004 as a legitimate and highly specialised bare-bones business wholesaling fossils primarily to museums around the world. The products that they trade in, though, rarely come out of the ground intact or ready to be displayed. They often need work. And that's what they do here: they reassemble bones, touch up and clean them, piece them together, and create displays of million-year-old creatures.

The Dinosaur Lab is the brainchild of Carly Burbank and her husband Terry Ciotka, who have both been working with fossils for decades. It's actually a three-part business: a working restoration lab, an educational destination, and a one-of-a-kind gift shop with some really unique and interesting specimens and minerals.

At the beginning, Burbank and Ciotka did their work behind closed doors, but after years of urging from family, friends, and clients, they decided to go public. Now anyone can see how these bones are restored and then assembled to museum display quality. Most museums have strict rules on touching displays, but you can touch things here. Some of the bones have magnets embedded in them, so you can pluck off a dino's rib and hold it in your hands. You can book a 90-minute tour of the facility, which includes half an hour of hands-on work, when you get to excavate real dinosaur fossils with your own hands.

Address 491 Dupplin Road #2, Victoria, BC V8Z 1B8, +1 (778) 966-3466, www.dinolabinc.ca | Getting there Bus 21, 22 to Burnside at Washington, turn right onto Dupplin Road, then walk 4 minutes | Hours Daily 10am–4:30pm, reservations required | Tip Offbeat Hotel Zed in the same neighbourhood has a wild colour scheme, comic books in every room, an old VW Van permanently parked out front, a great restaurant called The Ruby, and the Zedinator, a three-story-high, bubble-gum-pink water slide jutting out of the hotel balcony (3110 Douglas Street, www.hotelzed.com).

36 The Dominion Astrophysical Observatory

The Centre of the Universe

Ask any Western Canadian where the Centre of the Universe is, and the sarcastic answer will likely be "Toronto." Ask any Victorian, and you may be surprised with their response. An often overlooked and wonderful old astrological observatory in Saanich, billed itself as the "Centre of the Universe," and it has certainly earned the right to make that boastful global assertion.

Installed in 1918, The Dominion Astrophysical Observatory's 72-inch reflecting Plaskett Telescope was the world's largest – almost. Its huge mirror disc alone weighed 1,970 kilos (4,340 pounds) and had to be shipped from Belgium just before the outbreak of World War I. But it was scratched in the manufacturing process and had to be reground twice. That, combined with the war, delayed its delivery. Placing it into the brand new, double-walled, steel observatory was a monumental task. A horse-drawn wagon was used to slowly haul it to the top of the steep road on Little Saanich Mountain.

The Plaskett Telescope finally saw its first twinkling starlight shine through its cutting-edge lens on May 6th, 1918. In the meantime, another official American observatory telescope beat Victoria to the punch – barely. Six months earlier in 1917, the 100-inch Hooker Telescope was set up near Los Angeles. Today, the old 73 and 100-inch refractors don't mean that much. In order to put both telescopes' contributions to science into perspective, it's important to note that at the time, most observatories were using 19th-century technology, with 12 to 24-inch refractors.

As you drive to the observatory, notice the beautiful building itself. Its design is right out of a *Flash Gordon* movie, and since 800 tons of concrete went into its construction, it is likely to last for light years.

Address 5071 West Saanich Road, Victoria, BC V9E 2E7, +1 (250) 363-3638, www.centreoftheuniverse.org/visiting-the-hill, info@centreoftheuniverse.org | **Getting there** Bus 83 to West Saanich at Observatory | **Hours** Mon–Fri 9:15am–5pm, see website for event schedule and to book a tour | **Tip** Quarky Science is a great science store in Victoria that sells telescopes, and its goal is to make science interesting, fun, and accessible to people of all ages (8550 East Saanich Road, www.quarkyscience.ca).

37 The Duck Building

Wagons, women, and walls

This building has seen it all, and you should see it while you can. Simeon Duck (1834–1905), the proprietor of Duck's Carriage Works – the first wagon and carriage maker in the city – had this building built in 1892. Duck had arrived in Victoria some 30 years earlier, having figured out that selling provisions to prospectors was more profitable than being one. All those carriages you see in old photos of miners hauling supplies and equipment from Victoria to the Cariboo were made here by Duck.

But later on, when Duck was in his mid-sixties, he decided to rent his building to Ms. Stella Carroll, a 28-year-old madam from California.

Carroll came from San Francisco and knew from experience there was money to be made selling rides of a different kind. She sub-rented rooms on the upper floors to young ladies and operated as their "landlady." She furnished the main floor parlour area with luxury and style, and she provided music, food, and booze, and the men were drawn in like bees to honey. They paid handsomely for meals and refreshments, and the ladies charged handsomely for their attentions – and Stella made a killing on "rent."

The building was designed by architect William Tuff Whiteway (1856–1940), best known for building the iconic Sun Tower on Vancouver's Pender Street and is on the Canadian Heritage Building Registry. In time, it was purchased by Victoria businessman Michael Williams, who left the building and more to the University of Victoria. With a business partner, UVic plans to convert it into a hotel stretching nearly a full block along Broad Street, with two infill buildings on either side of Duck's original façade. UVic Properties will retain ownership of the land and receive annual revenue through a 99-year lease. Duck's is the building that keeps making its owners rich. Maybe give it a rub for good luck.

Address 1314 Broad Street, Victoria, BC V8W 2A9 | Getting there Bus 10, 24, 25 to Johnson at Broad | Hours Unrestricted from the outside only | Tip A few steps away is a more modern building built in 1949 as the Victoria headquarters of the Bank of Toronto. Today, it is home to the University of Victoria's Legacy Art Gallery (630 Yates Street, www.uvic.ca/legacygalleries).

38__The Dutch Bakery

Where the melting pot includes butter

Nothing is more fundamentally Canadian than the Dutch Bakery story. Canada's recipe for success has relied on hard-working immigrants contributing their skills, talents, and traditions to this amazing multicultural nation. It's a story that's been repeated for decades from coast to coast to coast, and it often starts with the same simple narrative: A Canadian immigrant family sponsors another immigrant family from their home country to come live here.

In 1955, a Dutch family living in Victoria sponsored Kees and Mabel Schaddelee to settle in their hometown of Victoria. The Schaddelees ran a bakery in Rotterdam, so when they arrived here, they found work at a local bakery. They later opened their own diner in Victoria, the Dutch Bakery. They had four sons, who all worked at the diner. Those sons had kids, and eight of those kids ended up working at the Dutch Bakery too.

Traditional family values and European pride run deep. Long-time local customers attest that everything here still tastes fresh, authentic, and delicious. It's no wonder since the family has been running it for over 65 years. The yummy baked goods are made with traditional Dutch recipes passed down from generations. The old, tattered recipe book they came from started falling apart years ago and has been photocopied over and over again. The almond paste is made in house, and the buttercream and tart shells are made with real butter. Everything there is made from scratch. The old-fashioned glass bakery cases have so much to offer it's hard to leave the place without taking something with you.

The Dutch Bakery's hot-pink to-go cardboard boxes have attended more dinner parties and receptions in Victoria than you can shake a windmill at. With only 65 seats, the retro style diner fills up quickly for breakfast and lunch. Wooden shoes are optional.

Address 718 Fort Street, Victoria, BC V8W 1H2, +1 (250) 385-1012, www.thedutchbakery.com, dutchbakeryvictoria@gmail.com | Getting there Bus 3, 6, 11, 14, 15 to Fort at Douglas | Hours Diner: Tue–Sat 8am–3pm; bakery 8am–4pm | Tip Russell Books, Canada's largest independent bookstore, is right across the street with 1,672 square metres (18,000 square feet) of space housing a million books (100–747 Fort Street, www.russellbooks.com).

39 Empress 1908 Gin Distillery

Purple reign

Purple-hued Empress 1908 Gin, handcrafted in small batch copper-pot stills, is inspired by the legendary Fairmont Empress Hotel in downtown Victoria. On top of traditional botanicals, they've added a signature blend of black tea, like the tea served at the Empress Hotel, and butterfly pea blossom, "an exotic herb that balances the traditional citrus notes of gin with a warm herbal earthiness." The butterfly pea blossom not only adds flavour, but it also adds colour. This flower is responsible for the purple colour (actually indigo) of this regal refreshment.

The flower, known as the Asian pigeonwing, originates in Southeast Asia and has some of the nutritional benefits typical of other richly blue-coloured foods, like blueberries. It contains a high amount of anthocyanins which are a type of antioxidant. In traditional Ayurvedic medicine, tea made from the flower is sometimes used as a memory enhancer and sedative agent, and as a treatment for stress, anxiety, and depression. Whether those properties still work when distilled into gin is anyone's guess, but now you know a lot more about the butterfly pea flower.

You can see how all of this comes together when you visit Victoria Distillers' seaside distillery. Engineers and environmentalists will also enjoy seeing how they use a closed-loop energy system that recaptures heat from the water and delivers it to the nearby Sidney Pier Hotel. Through the use of their geothermal system, the distillery saves about 7,000 litres (1,500 gallons) of water and transfers 850,000 BTUs of energy to the hotel with every distillation. This energy keeps the hotel rooms warm, reduces its carbon footprint, and conserves precious water. So, enjoy this gin and be healthy and green, while drinking purple.

Address 9891 Seaport Place, Sidney, BC V8L 4X3, +1 (250) 544-8217, www.empressgin.com/victoria-distillers | Getting there Bus 81, 82, 83, 85, 87, 88 to James White Boulevard at Fifth | Hours Wed–Sun noon–6pm | Tip The Sidney Fishing Pier is a pleasant, six-minute walk along a scenic seawall path that features an iconic wooden pier and delivers awesome views, sculptures, and refreshing greenery along the way (at the east end of Bevan Avenue, Sidney).

40 The Empress Hotel's Centennial Garden

Home to 30,000 bees and one marmot

When you slather delicious honey on your freshly baked scone during Afternoon Tea at the Empress Hotel, here is something to ponder. Did the bees gather it from the decorative floral arrangements on the BC Legislature grounds, from the wide variety of plants in Beacon Hill Park, or from the beautiful flowers at the Abkhazi Garden?

Since bees can fly up to 5 kilometres (3 miles) when they go out on their nectar foraging trips, the honey could have come from any one of those bucolic attractions, or from an endless number of similar Victoria locations. Or the bees may have simply gathered the nectar from right in front of their own four-box hive, which sits in the lovely Centennial Garden on the grounds of the hotel close by. The Empress Hotel, which has welcomed different queens and kings from around the world over the years, has its very own Queen Bee. She lives here in that hive year-round with about 30,000 of her daughters, and they produce the honey that supplies the hotel's restaurants. In May of 2011, the hotel started their bee program, which now yields hundreds of pounds of honey each year.

As you venture outside to admire the hive, you may run into another permanent resident of Centennial Garden. Roger the Marmot has lived there since before the bees arrived. He moved here in 2008 and takes his name from one of the hotel's former managers. Roger is a yellow-bellied marmot, and he may be from Alberta originally. Although you'll find lots of marmots on the Island, the yellow-bellied species is not indigenous, so how he got here is a mystery. For years, he has enjoyed a steady diet of the foliage around him, and he also likes carrots and celery. He seems to enjoy the attention from all the tourists who come by and say hello.

Address 721 Government Street, Victoria, BC V8W 1W5, +1 (250) 384 8111, www.fairmont.com/empress-victoria | **Getting there** Bus 10 to Wharf at Broughton, or bus 1, 2, 3, 5, 27 to Douglas at Humboldt | **Hours** Unrestricted | **Tip** A company with an interesting name, Babe's Honey, has been tending bees and selling honey in Victoria since 1945 (Galey Market, 4150 Blenkinsop Road, Saanich, www.babes-honey-farm.com).

41 Fairway to Heaven

Victoria's haunted golf club

"The Victoria Golf Club, founded in 1893, is the oldest 18-hole golf course in Canada in its original location, and second oldest in North America," states the website. Situated on 94 acres on Gonzales Point, the course overlooks the Strait of Juan de Fuca. From here, distracted golfers can often see otters, seals, orcas, and even the United States on a clear day. It is undoubtedly one of the world's most scenic places to play golf. Even shock rock legend, and notorious golf monster Alice Cooper has played here. But did Cooper know the fairway on the seventh hole was once a crime scene? Maybe he got chills while humming along to his hit tune "Welcome to My Nightmare." In any case, on the evening of September 22, 1936, a local nurse, Doris Gravlin, 30 years old and with eyes like David Bowie, went for a walk on the links and never came back.

Five days later a caddy from the club went looking for an errant golf ball and stumbled across Gravlin's body among the rocks, grass, and logs on the beach that runs next to the course. She had been murdered. A month later, her husband Victor's dead body was found tangled in kelp and floating near the ninth tee. Police assumed Victor had killed Doris and then drowned himself.

The first sightings of Doris' ghost began shortly after her death. Over time, there would be so many stories of sightings that she soon gained notoriety as Victoria's most famous and most active ghost. She has been seen in her dated 1930s attire, and she has been seen gliding across the ground in a glowing white dress. Legend has it that if a young couple saw her, they would break up. After all, marriage was not good to Doris. Another tale says that Doris' ghost wouldn't rest until her son – seven years old at the time of her death – was told the truth about her murder. The truth was kept from him until he was 67 years old. She hasn't been seen since.

Address 1110 Beach Drive, Victoria, BC V8S 2M9, +1 (250) 598-4321, www.victoriagolf.com | Getting there Bus 1, 2 to Central at Newport | Hours Unrestricted | Tip Visit the hidden Oak Bay Native Plant Garden (1178 Beach Drive, www.oakbay.ca).

42 Fake Fisherman's Hut
Cleverly camouflaged, top-secret searchlight

Formally known as Searchlight Emplacement No. 7, this artillery searchlight structure is a remarkable and very unique relic of World War II. The most interesting aspect of it is that it has been camouflaged to look like a fisherman's hut, complete with a derelict rowboat stashed in front. It's painted to look like a wooden structure, which is obvious if you're standing right in front of it. But if you were in a submarine out on the Strait of Juan de Fuca peeking at it through a periscope or gazing at it through binoculars from the deck of a battleship, you'd easily see a humble hut and direct your fire elsewhere. Behind the fake façade, between the two false windows, is a metal door that opens on rollers to reveal one of the biggest light bulbs you've ever seen: a 152-centimetre (60-inch) General Electric Type B capable of lighting up a target miles away.

The artillery battery here dates back to 1895, but American visitors can rest assured that, while the artillery guns are pointing directly toward Port Angeles just to the south, the guns and searchlights added in the 1940s were placed there to defend Victoria, Vancouver, and even Seattle from their common enemy across the Pacific. Above the innocent-looking fisherman's hut, you'll see the Belmont Battery, with its grey, quick-firing, twelve-pounder guns, twin-barrelled six-pounder guns, and a tower station that would direct fire. At night, those guns and the tower would coordinate with the searchlight to defend the area.

By the end of the war, there was a string of searchlights along the coastline, about seventeen just along the Victoria-Esquimalt Fortress area. This one and others at Fort Rodd were initially powered by diesel engines and managed through a central fortified Searchlight Engine Room. Not many survive, and few are as interesting as this one, which is a designated Federal Heritage Building.

Address 603 Fort Rodd Hill Road, Victoria, BC V9C 2W8 | Getting there Bus 43 to College at Thetis | Hours Oct 16–Apr 30 10–4pm; May 1–Oct 15 10–5pm | Tip Walk a few paces to the northeast along the path to find the brass marker commemorating the iconic Canadian Arctic Expedition, which sailed from this point in 1913. Immediately to the east, across the water, see if you can spot the Bickford Signal Tower.

43 _ The Fireside Grill

Farm to table food, and some very unusual spirits

The Fireside Grill is universally recognized today for its fine dining, its patio, and happy hours. But it is also highly ranked on the spooko-meter. This stunning Tudor Revival-style building, constructed in the 1930s, is built on a number of what spiritualists call ley lines, which are sort of like latitude and longitude lines but full of cosmic energy that heightens spiritual and paranormal activity.

The theory that ley lines ran between prehistoric, Roman, and mediaeval places was popularised by Alfred Watkins in his 1922 book *Early British Trackways, Moats, Mounds, Camps and Sites*. Watkins theorised that ancient Brits travelled in straight lines between sacred sites, and he connected places like Stonehenge to the Pyramids. It sounds like tinfoil-hat stuff to most people, but many present-day students of Earth Mysteries and such still think there's something to it. Some people also say the ley lines might be navigational beacons for visiting spaceships, or maybe an under-ground cosmic railway for spirits.

One of the Grill's first owners was Katharine Maltwood, who also happened to be a student of the occult. She was a progressive and exciting personality of her era and amused herself and her friends with her studies in Egyptian culture, Masonic rituals, Goddess spirit-uality, and Theosophy. She wrote books about King Arthur and the zodiac. Maltwood lived here from 1938 to 1961 with her husband John and amassed a considerable collection of antiques from their travels in Europe and Asia, which were later donated with the house to the University of Victoria. That she loved the place is irrefutable. That she was drawn to it through its cosmic energy is possible. That she haunts it to this day is a matter you will have to decide for your-self while you enjoy something off the classic brunch menu featuring three kinds of eggs benedict and a classic croque madame.

FIRESIDE GRILL

ENTRANCE

Address 4509 West Saanich Road, Victoria, BC V8Z 3G1, +1 (250) 479-1222,
www.firesidegrill.com | Getting there Bus 6, 31, 32 to West Saanich at Elk Lake Drive |
Hours Mon–Thu 11:30am–8pm, Fri 11:30am–9pm, Sat 10:30am–9pm, Sun 10:30am–8pm |
Tip The Maltwood Gallery, a legacy of John and Katherine Maltwood, is located at
the Mearns Centre at the bottom level of the University of Victoria's McPherson Library
(99111 Ring Road, www.maltwood.uvic.ca).

44 First Rogers' Chocolates
Sweet and tragic

When exactly Charles "Candy" Rogers made his first chocolates is a bit of a mystery, though it is well established that the sweet-toothed, American grocer arrived in Victoria in 1885 at age 31. He met and married his wife Leah in 1888, and their son Frederick was born two years later. Charles did well enough in his first few years of business, and he was able to acquire this first stunning chocolate shop location, across the street from the original grocery store. As he moved into the fancy new shop, Rogers did what so many of us long to do: he said goodbye to cabbages and carrots, and hello to chocolates! Ever since that day, Rogers' Chocolate Shop has been the crown jewel in the Rogers chocolate empire. And the only greens Rogers saw again were green dollar bills.

The shop still has the original stained-glass windows, pristine tile work, and polished wooden shelves that wowed customers' eyeballs just as well as the displays wooed their tongues. Rogers' is the oldest chocolate company in Western Canada and the first in British Columbia. It may also be Canada's most haunted chocolate shop.

The story goes that, in 1905, their teenage son, who apparently had more interest in TNT than truffles, shot himself dead at the New England Hotel after accidentally blowing three of his fingers off a few months earlier. Seeking solace in work and comfort in each other's company, Charles and Leah burned the midnight oil in the kitchen of the chocolate shop, sometimes even staying overnight, even though they could well afford not to.

They carried on relentlessly, even developing a mail order business to satisfy chocolate lovers around the world. Charles died in 1927, and Leah continued to run the business until she followed him to the grave in 1952. Some say the two restless workaholics still drop in and visit the shop at night and move things around.

Address 913 Government Street, Victoria, BC V8W 1X5, +1 (250) 881-8771, www.rogerschocolates.com | **Getting there** Bus 10 to Wharf at Broughton | **Hours** Mon–Sat 10am–10pm, Sun 11am–8pm | **Tip** The New England Hotel building where Frederick tragically shot himself is a short walk away (1312 Government Street).

45 — The Fisgard Lighthouse
The sad tale of one oar

As you approach the Fisgard Lighthouse, you will probably wonder whether this place was built to act as a navigational beacon to guide ships, or was it purposely created to allow artists to paint it, photographers to shoot it, and poets to write about it. It's a stunningly beautiful building and a quintessential West Coast must-see. The red-brick, gothic-influenced tower, built in 1860, may also prompt you to ponder the idyllic lives enjoyed by the different lighthouse keepers who lived here. The breathtaking views of the ocean and the Olympic Mountains conjure up words like *peaceful*, *quiet*, and *serene*. The word *dangerous* is not likely to come to mind.

The Fisgard Lighthouse and its sister Race Rocks Lighthouse, built at the same time, were a big deal. Vancouver Island was part of the British colonies then, and the British Government made the political commitment and investment to aid naval vessels and merchant ships entering the harbour during the busy American Goldrush, when 25,000 miners descended upon the region. The cast-iron spiral staircase inside is worth the climb. It was built in sections in San Francisco and shipped north.

To get to the lighthouse today, you can walk from the parking lot to the 17-metre (56-foot) tower. However, had you visited before 1951, you would have needed a rowboat. That year, a short causeway was built to connect the small, jagged island to the mainland, allowing the lighthouse keeper to get provisions more conveniently. But years earlier, on July 3, 1898, an empty rowboat with just one oar in it was found near the lighthouse. The waters between the lighthouse and the shore can get choppy and rough. Searchers eventually found the drowned body of lighthouse keeper John Dare. You can still see his rowboat *The Rosina* next to the lighthouse, with a plaque attached to it that reads, *A lost oar meant a lost life.*

Address 603 Fort Rodd Hill Road, Victoria, BC V9C 2W8, www.pc.gc.ca/en/lhn-nhs/bc/fortroddhill | Getting there By car, take Trans-Canada Highway at Highway 1 to exit 10 for Island Highway towards View Royal and Colwood. Continue for about 3 kilometres (1.8 miles) and turn left at Ocean Boulevard. Follow the Parks Canada directional signage till you arrive at the free parking lot. | Hours Daily Oct 16–Apr 30 10am–4pm; May 1–Oct 15 10am–5pm | Tip Just south on Ocean Boulevard is Esquimalt Lagoon is a long, beautiful spit with driftwood art, amazing views of Mount Baker, summer food trucks, and long sandy beaches. Many people think it's Victoria's best lagoon (www.colwood.ca/discover).

46 Folk Art Fence

Metchosin's wacky, whimsical, wonderful wall

For a polar opposite change from the busy Inner Harbour in the hectic downtown core, head out to the farming community of Metchosin. It's a lovely, sparsely populated district with wide-open spaces, lots of Arbutus and Garry oak trees, farms on the ocean, and winding rural roads leading past small forests and secluded rural homes. Lots of artists live in Metchosin, and there is a quirky piece of folk art that has been grabbing the locals' attention for the last decade. It's a fence that's decorated, painted, and curated to tell a number of different local stories. Or you can interpret the 100 metres (109 yards) of creativity sprawled out on the side of a road anyway you wish.

The artist Janice Poulin, who sadly passed away in 2021, was a long-time Metchosin resident. Her parents owned the town general store. When she and her husband Eugene, who still lives there, replaced the old wire fence on their property with a new wooden one, she saw the fence as a giant, 3D canvas.

Starting from the north end, you'll see many old household items nailed to the fence under the heading, *Remnants from the Past*. Next, you'll come across a tribute to the Garry oak tree with a short description, which is then followed by a display of Chilcotin wood. Then a group of teapots, cups, and other antique China hang suspended in mid-air. Farther along is a leather horse next to several folksy birdhouses. Get ready for some bird-watching next, this time cormorants that you will spot in a diorama through a window.

An old bench leads to a display of rusting spare car parts, including vintage taillights, rear view mirrors, and gauges. Poulin's father collected steel chains, and some of them are hung next to a poem about him. There are many more wonderful parts of the fence to see, and the very last panel simply reads, *This is Metchosin, fields, forests, beach, sky and fresh air.*

Address 579 Witty Beach Road, Victoria, BC V9C 4H8 | Getting there Bus 55 to Metchosin at Witty Beach | Hours Unrestricted | Tip Just down the road from the fence, you'll find Bilston Creek Farm, a lavender farm rich in local history dating back to 1851. Its gift shop sells lavender-related items (4185 Metchosin Road, www.bilston.ca).

47 __FOO Asian Street Food
Everything in a bowl or a box

There are no fancy china teacups at FOO Asian Street Food because this is not a fancy restaurant. It's gritty, it's located in a parking lot, it's overshadowed by brick buildings from yesteryear, and it has an unspectacular view of Blanchard Street. But what it does have is big-city urban vibes and a menu of Asian food created by a Cordon Bleu chef, who knows exactly what he's doing. Chef Patrick Lynch spent a year travelling across Asia – Australia, New Zealand, Cambodia, Vietnam, Thailand, Malaysia, Sri Lanka, and more – eating from food trucks and carts and making scrupulous notes on what to prepare for his own restaurant in Victoria. Then he brought all those experiences and sensations back here. Everything is created to be served in a bowl or a box.

With co-owner Sterling Grice, Lynch has created a unique restaurant that serves up the taste of Asia and delivers a helping of authentic street-food vibes as well. The restaurant was at the edge of downtown when it first opened, but the location is now considered fairly central. People from all walks enjoy the food. You might be seated next to a student from the University of Victoria or a legendary rock icon. It's true – Lynch once served a bowl of food to Canadian music legend Randy Bachman of The Guess Who and Bachman Turner Overdrive. You know that guy has taste!

When you walk into FOO, you're also walking into a bit of Victoria history. The name is an homage to one of Victoria's legendary restaurants, Foo Hong, which closed just as Lynch and Grice were making their plans. The building itself dates back over a hundred years and was once the carriage house for the Dominion Hotel, here since 1880. Since then, the carriage house has been a service station and, when the current owners took it over in 2009, a refrigerated, walk-in-walk-out beer store. Just another reason why it's so cool to eat here.

Address 769 Yates Street, Victoria, BC V8W 1L6, +1 (250) 383-3111, www.foofood.ca |
Getting there Bus 4, 6, 7, 11, 22 to Douglas at View | Hours Daily 11:30am–10pm |
Tip The nearby Carnegie Library, built in 1904, was featured on a Canadian postage stamp
in 1996 and is considered one of the city's finest civic public works (794 Yates Street).

48 __ Fort Victoria's Well

The Rithet Building's watery wonder

It was out of sight for over a century, and it's still behind closed doors. But you can poke your nose through the Rithet Building's big yellow doors and cast your eyes on the well that once served Fort Victoria's earliest traders and residents.

It was built around the same time as the fort (1843) but then fell into disuse around 1870, when water was pumped into town from Elk Lake. Before long it was boarded over, and a building was built over it. Being out of sight meant out of mind. It was not rediscovered until 1978, when the Province of British Columbia bought the buildings and began to restore them for office use. During the restoration process, they uncovered the original well, complete with a mechanical pump. Now you too can take a gander at this formerly watery wonder.

The well is fascinating, but so is the building around it. The Rithet Building is named for Scottish-born entrepreneur R. P. Rithet, part owner of the Albion Iron Works. It was built in four stages between 1861 and 1889 and embodies the early evolution of the city, illustrating how new technology supported the growth of Victoria from fur-trading post to thriving commercial centre. The use of cast-iron columns made in San Francisco on the earliest part of the building reflect the growing trade links with the United States. Rithet's Albion Iron Works company provided the cast-iron columns for the newest sections of the building. After he bought the building in 1888, he ran his mercantile and insurance company from it until 1948.

Access to the rear of the building via Helmcken Alley is also important, as it retains the network of Klondike-era courtyards and alleyways that are trademarks of Victoria's historic infrastructure. It's fun to visit the well and think about which figures from Victoria's nineteenth-century past may have also stood near this spot to quench their thirst.

Address 1117 Wharf Street, Victoria, BC V8W 1T4 | Getting there Bus 14, 15 to Fort at Wharf | Hours Unrestricted | Tip Further down Wharf Street, look for the old Custom House building, where every gold prospector making their way to the Yukon stopped to get their paperwork in order (1002 Wharf Street).

49 Freeloading Freighters
Hey! That one's from Liberia!

If you enjoy watching ships near the shore and imagining where they came from and where they are going, Victoria is a great place for that. After all, it's surrounded by water. The Port of Victoria waterways welcome cruise ships, tour boats, ferries, tugboats, barges, kayaks, canoes, yachts, and other recreational watercraft year-round. In recent years, the harbour has started to see more enormous freighters just floating out there, seemingly doing nothing. They are actually peacefully floating in the water, waiting for a spot to open up at the Vancouver port so they can unload.

They may stay there for two days or as long as a month, anchored in the same place, easy to spot. Victoria is not a freighter container port, so it's reasonable to wonder what the story is with these vessels. They are waiting to go to Vancouver, which is a major West Coast container port.

When they get to Vancouver, where parking is at a premium, they unload their cargo, turn around, and go back to where they came from to get more containers to bring back. Some of the freighters that you will see in the Victoria waters carry grain and coal, but most of them just have a massive number of colourful, rectangular, Lego-style boxed containers stacked four or five high on their decks. And the decks are huge, up to the length of three football fields. The containers you see on board the freighters come in 20 and 40-foot lengths. The average number of containers onboard each freighter is about 15,000, while the larger ships, which you may also see in the waters off Victoria, can hold up to 24,000 boxes.

One of the best places to admire these massive maroon, purple, or orange-coloured engineering beauties is at Perimeter Park 1, which is on a hill in Colwood just off Metchosin Road, with views out onto Royal Bay. Bring your binoculars to record the ships' names and their flags of origin.

Address Perimeter Park 1, Gratton Road just past Perimeter Place, Colwood, BC V9C 4J6, www.colwood.ca | Getting there Bus 52, 55, 59 to Metchosin at Cotlow | Hours Unrestricted | Tip Nearby Sequoia Coffee is built out of old freighter shipping containers (3582 Quarry Street, Colwood, www.facebook.com/sequoiacoastalcoffee).

50__ The Galloping Goose Trail
An easy hike into history

British Columbians are addicted to hiking and biking. Vancouver has the famous Stanley Park Seawall (10km/6.2 miles), Whistler has the adventurous Valley Trail (42km/26 miles), and Victoria has the historical Galloping Goose (55km/34.2 miles). What makes the Galloping Goose (or simply the Goose, as the locals call it) so special is its lineage that can be traced back to 1922, when it was not a trail but a railroad track that ran trains daily between Sooke and Victoria. That explains why the trail is so wide, as trains require a wide berth. It's also why the grade never gets too steep here, as trains travel best on flat terrain. But what can't be so easily explained is the trail's crazy name. After all, geese don't gallop – they waddle.

The company that operated the passenger and lumber-transporting railway line was called the Rio Grande Southern Railroad, which went bankrupt in 1931. To reduce business operating expenses, they abandoned their costly steam-powered locomotives. They replaced them with a quirky, strange looking hybrid cross between a rickety Beverly Hillbillies-style vehicle and a train. Basically, a converted gas-engine automobile was morphed into a gawky and noisy rail car called the Galloping Goose. One story is that the name originated from the sound the car's horn made, as opposed to a train's usual distinctive whistle.

History aside, what can you expect today walking or riding on this bucolic trail in the middle of a West Coast rainforest? Since it was once a railroad, expect to cross some impressive bridges. Don't expect to come across any galloping geese though, as the wildlife and farm life you are likely to see includes rabbits, deer, eagles, pigs, sheep, and horses. The hard-packed trail is easy to hike and surrounded by foxgloves, blackberry bushes, shasta daisies, and salal. You'll also come across Douglas fir, Arbutus, hemlock, and cedar trees.

Address The trail begins at the south end of the Selkirk Trestle, at the foot of Alston Street in Victoria West, www.gallopinggoosetrail.com | Getting there Bus 48, 54, 55, 64 to Happy Valley or bus 14 to Skinner at Catherine | Hours Unrestricted | Tip If you need some good hiking shoes, walking poles, or comfortable clothes to hike the Goose, then check out Robinson's Outdoor Store, a family run business that has been the premier source for outdoor gear in Victoria for 91 years (1307 Broad Street, www.robinsonsoutdoors.com).

51 The Giant Sequoia
British Columbia's official Christmas tree

Forestry is still BC's largest industry, so it is not surprising to find a big, beautiful tree proudly towering above the stately Victoria legislative buildings. One particular tree is worth seeing and admiring for a few reasons.

It is a sequoia tree. This type of tree is a bit unusual and seems almost out of place here. Also known as California redwoods or by the old British name Wellingtonia trees, sequoias are not native to British Columbia. They can, however, be successfully transplanted and grown here. This one put down its roots in 1863 and is still growing. And growing at a rate of about 30 cm (1 foot) a year, it stands well over 30 metres (100 feet).

The second thing that makes the tree interesting is its official status. Most provinces have an official flower, bird, and crest. This sequoia is British Columbia's Official Christmas Tree. Be wary of flashy imposter trees lurking around the capitol during the festive season; this one's the real deal. During the month of December, it lives up to its auspicious title when it's adorned with thousands of colourful lights. Every year, the tree participates in an annual, nationally coordinated celebration called "Christmas Lights Across Canada," which sees important Christmas trees across the nation lit at the same time.

The tree's exact location has historical significance as well. Before the present-day Legislature was completed in 1898, a series of six smaller, less fortified colonial administrative buildings known as the Bird Cages sat where the tree stands today. Built in 1859, the long-gone buildings were described by the *Victoria Gazette* as a mixture of "Chinese pagodas, Swiss cottages and Italian-villa fancy bird cages."

Sequoias like the one on the Legislative grounds live up to 2,000 years, so there is really no rush for you to get down to the inner harbour to see it.

Address 501 Belleville Street, Victoria, BC V8V 1X4 www.leg.bc.ca/learn-about-us/
visiting-the-legislature | Getting there Bus 32, 42, 48, 53, 61, 65 to Legislature Terminal |
Hours Unrestricted | Tip The nearby Royal BC Museum Native Plant Garden is home to t
he province's largest and most diverse collection of native plants. Walking through the small,
admission-free gardens, you will see over 400 different native species (675 Belleville Street,
www.royalbcmuseum.bc.ca/visit/exhibitions/native-plant-garden).

52 Glass Beach
Sea gems

Most parks or recreational areas you visit have strict rules on taking home anything you find, like plants, rocks, little critters, etc. A beautiful outdoor location in Sidney offers a refreshing different policy on ecological pilfering. It's a place with an abundance of hidden treasures that are just waiting to be found and taken home. It's called Glass Beach, and up until now it's been a well-kept secret. As the name suggests, it's where you'll find no shortage of small pieces of glass that have been tumbled by the sea for decades, turning them into shiny, smooth gems. The seashore is teeming with these special little souvenirs that look great back at home in a dish or bowl, or sitting on a window ledge. You can even just leave a few in a drawer or keep one or two in your pocket for luck.

As you stroll along on Glass Beach, looking down as you walk, you may find yourself wondering, where did all these translucent jewels come from? There are several different theories and stories. The first one is that long ago, household garbage, including old bottles and glass containers, was simply dumped into the ocean nearby. Organic garbage, food scraps, and things like paper and wood deteriorated over time, but the glass got smashed and rolled on the rocks over the decades, breaking into smaller and smaller pieces.

Another story attributes the origin of the petite, overlooked, and weathered jewels to an old mill that used to be located on Beacon Avenue. It burned down in 1936, and much of it, including glass windows, was washed into the churning sea. That same churning sea has also caused a shipwreck or two. Since ships carried glass cargo a century ago, this too is a very plausible explanation. Some of the antique pieces of glass found on the beach have been traced to a large manufacturer called San Francisco and Pacific Glassworks, which dates back to 1876.

Address 2533 Beacon Avenue West, Sidney, BC V8L 1Y2 | Getting there Bus 70, 71, 72, 81, 85, 87, 88 to Fifth at Beacon | Hours Unrestricted | Tip Just south of Glass Beach is Divers Point, where you'll see a double-sized sculpture by Alan C. Porter of a scuba diver with a bright yellow air tank, just across from the Sidney Hotel Waterfront Inn and Spa (9775 First Street, Sidney).

53_ Goldstream Park Salmon
The circle of life

Pacific salmon come back each year to spawn and then die at the same spot where they were born. Witnessing the colourful chum species, with their distinctive hooked jaws, swim upstream to lay their eggs is a wonderful way to spend part of a crisp and cool fall day. Serious wildlife observing often requires arduous hikes, a knowledge of the area, and patience. That's not the case with the salmon spawning at Goldstream though. The river is easy to find, not far from town, and the fish are a short walk from the parking lot. The best time to go see this natural phenomenon is between mid-October and the end of December. But you can visit the park year-round and enjoy its scenic waterfalls, meandering rivers, interesting West Coast flora and fauna, and lots of birdlife.

Before you go, it helps to have a bit of background on the incredible salmon lifecycle. They generally spend their juvenile years in rivers and lakes and migrate out to the ocean for their adult lives, when they gain most of their body mass. Upon reaching maturity, they return home. The big question is around their uncanny ability to make it back to the exact same river or stream where they were born after venturing thousands of miles. They use something called magnetoreception, which is a sense they innately must detect the Earth's magnetic field, to find the river. Once they are in their home river, they use their sense of smell to detect where they were born years prior.

Because the Goldstream River gets quite shallow in some spots, it is interesting to stand on its banks and observe a female salmon digging a trench for her eggs. She accomplishes this by turning her body from side to side over and over again, displacing the gravel in the riverbed before she lays the eggs. Unfortunately, the salmon's health rapidly deteriorates in the fresh river water, and shortly after spawning they die.

Address 3450 Trans-Canada Highway, Victoria, BC V9B 5T9, www.goldstreampark.com |
Getting there By car, take Trans-Canada Highway/BC-1 N till you see the wooden sign at the
entrance to Goldstream Park | Hours Unrestricted | Tip On the other side of the highway there
is an easy 45-minute (round trip) hike to a local waterfall with a famous misleading name. From
the Goldstream Visitor Centre in the parking lot follow the short trail to a tunnel under the
highway that leads to Niagara Falls (2930 Trans-Canada Highway, www.goldstreampark.com).

54 Government Street Tattoo
The glorious On Hing Brothers Building

Canadian Prime Minister Justin Trudeau has a Haida raven tattoo, UK Prime Minister Winston Churchill had a ship's anchor tattoo, and US President Teddy Roosevelt had a family crest tattoo. So, if you want to be like these government leaders, there's no better place to get inked than on Government Street. But even if you don't want to get tats, you'll want to visit Government Street Tattoo because it features one of the most attractive storefronts in the entire city. Its brightly painted façade features red and gold paintwork and bold-serif font signage reminiscent of a nineteenth-century London umbrella shop or the magic and mystery of a painted gypsy caravan.

Behind the carnival paint is a fascinating peek at the history of Victoria. The building was constructed in 1897 for the prominent On Hing & Brothers Company by renowned and prolific architect Thomas Hooper. It has a "mixed use" design featuring commercial space on the ground floor and residences above. The multi-paned transom windows are a particularly noteworthy feature. The On Hing brothers were part of the wave of people who moved to Victoria in the late 1800s, chasing the opportunities of the Fraser Gold Rush of 1858, after chasing the gold in San Francisco. The brothers became prominent Chinatown landowners, and they purchased this lot, one of their earliest acquisitions, from the city's third mayor W. J. Macdonald for a princely $10,000.

When you stand on the sidewalk, look up and down the street and consider that this was once a muddy trail outside the eastern gate of Fort Victoria. The whole history of Victoria runs the length of this street. It has seen horse carts and the lively days of the Gold Rush, and it has been walked by just about every Canadian poet, author, artist, industrialist, politician, banker, lawyer, or merchant you care to mention. You can only wonder which of them might have had tattoos.

Address 1710 Government Street, Victoria, BC V8W 1Z5, +1 (250) 590-5379, www.governmentstreettattoo.com | **Getting there** Bus 14, 15, 24, 25 to Pandora at Government/Store | **Hours** Daily noon–6pm | **Tip** Snap out of your historic reverie and walk across the street to Smoking Lily, a modern women's clothing shop featuring "locally made clothes with an attitude" – silk screened originals all made in the shop from original designs (1713 Government Street, www.smokinglily.com).

55 The Hands of Victoria

Get a grip on art that's hip – on history

Victoria has a lot of great public art. Much of it, like that large statue of Queen Victoria outside the Legislature, is pretty hard to miss. But there's some art that's harder to find, and when you do find it, you have to scratch your head and wonder, "What's this all about?" *The Hands of Time* is one of those. And it's not even one piece of art … it's *twelve*.

One of the sculptures is a hand holding a mirror that reflects Victoria's Inner Harbour, which holds a key part of Victoria's history and identity. The reflection and text in the mirror, "I am here," reminds you that you're in the present, a result of all that has come before, and part of all that is yet to come. Further north and also near the water is a sculpture of hands tying a rope to a mooring ring. This one references the arrival of the first tall ships to the area. Original mooring rings – remnants of old Fort Victoria – are nearby.

Elsewhere, there are hands carrying books, carving a canoe paddle, cupping dogwood blossoms, digging camas bulbs, carrying point blankets, holding a railway spike, panning for gold, performing with a fan, and raising a cup of tea. The hands are located all around Victoria on buildings, lamp standards, rocks in landscaped areas, and on bedrock. Each of the three-dimensional, bronze hands is unique, varying in culture, age and gender, and designed to quietly convey significant elements, eras, and stories from Victoria's history.

The Hands were created by artist Crystal Przybille as part of the city's 150th Anniversary in 2012, hence the "12" theme. Przybille created 12 sculptures that represent the 12 numbers on the clock face, the 12 months in a year, and Victoria's sesquicentennial. If your feet want in on the action, the City of Victoria's website offers a map with the descriptions and locations the *Hands of Time* sculptures. Go on this self-guided walking tour to see them all.

I am here

Address Multiple locations, Victoria, BC, www.victoria.ca/EN/main/residents/culture/
public-art.html | Getting there Varies by location | Hours Unrestricted | Tip The Hands
at the Inner Harbour location are a stone's throw from the Victoria terminal for Harbour
Air and a great place to watch the float planes arrive.

56 Harrison Yacht Pond

Where you can be Master and Commander

If you'd like to have a 10-metre (34-foot) yacht or sailboat but can't afford one, there's a reasonably priced alternative: get yourself a model sailboat! At the Harrison Yacht Pond, you can be Master and Commander of your own yacht, sloop, schooner, or even a tugboat. You can even command a battleship or a submarine if that's more your style.

Named after George Holland, a sailor on the Hudson's Bay Company's doomed steamship SS *Beaver*, Holland Park is appropriately home to Harrison Yacht Pond, located at the bottom of Government Street at Dallas Road. Surrounded by a semicircle of trees, the kidney-shaped pond measures about 80 by 30 metres (260 by 100 feet) and is situated such that it takes full advantage of the winds that blow in from the ocean to power the model sailboats.

The modern history of the park goes back to the late 1940s, but the plaque erected at the sailing pond by the Victoria Model Ship Building Society (VMSS) states that the pond was dedicated in 1956 "...for the fun and enjoyment of model boating. Victorians and visitors alike." Since then, things have mostly been smooth sailing, but there has been occasional conflict. One source of trouble were the ducks and their earthbound, two-legged collaborators who insisted on feeding them here until they were shooed away. Another small conflict arose when motor-powered boats began to arrive on the scene. But the wind and motor factions have made their peace, and the seas are calm once again.

Before you take the plunge into this fascinating hobby, go to the pond, where you'll be able to get a better idea of what the sailing options are. You can chat with other land lubbers about the best way to get started. You can go at any time, but members of the Victoria Model Ship Building Society are here almost every Sunday morning, and that makes for fine viewing and conversation.

Address 561 Dallas Road, Victoria, BC V8V 1B2, www.vmss.ca | Getting there Bus 2, 3, 5 to Niagara at Menzies | Hours Unrestricted | Tip At the westernmost end of Holland Park, about 400 metres from the Pond, look for the stone marker which indicates this was once the site of a fortified Songhees village.

57___Hatley Castle
Victoria's movie star

In 1908, the elaborate Hatley Castle was built for James Dunsmuir, the son of former premier Robert Dunsmuir, lieutenant governor and the richest man in British Columbia. James Dunsmuir apparently once said, "Money doesn't matter. Just build what I want." Coincidentally, that same year, D. W. Griffith directed a silent, black-and-white movie called *Money Mad*. Money, movies, and the marvellous Hatley Castle would all go on to become intertwined in the years to come.

If you have never been to the absolutely amazing, sprawling, 40-room Scottish baronial-style mansion, chances are you have seen it in a movie or on TV. For decades, dozens of different shows have used it as a location set. The flowery fairy tale-like setting, with its sprawling Edwardian gardens, have been irresistible to producers of fantasy shows like *Deadpool*, *The Descendants*, and *Smallville*. The castle doubled as Professor Xavier's School of Gifted Youngsters in *The X-Men* movies, as Hatley Castle looks similar to Xavier's private estate in the *X-Men* comic books published by Marvel.

In the TV series *The Arrow*, Hatley Castle was used as the queen's mansion, and in *The Killing*, it doubled as St. George's Military Academy. In the hit 2011 film *The Descendants*, what you thought was Auradon Prep was actually Hatley Castle. If you ever watched the TV series *MacGyver* … well you get the picture. It is such a popular filming location that the well-known website www.TheTravel.com placed Hatley Castle on its list of the "10 Best Movie Locations Worth Travelling To."

Hatley Castle has one more business advantage going for it when it comes to attracting new productions. Budgets are important in the motion picture industry, and the Canadian dollar exchange rate, along with government subsidies, has fostered a thriving movie business in BC, where film productions spend over two billion dollars annually.

Address 2005 Sooke Road, Victoria, BC V9B 5Y2, +1 (250) 391-2666, www.hatleycastle.com |
Getting there Bus 39, 43, 48, 51, 52 to Sooke Road at Aldeane – Royal Roads U | Hours Daily
10am–5pm | Tip Craigdarroch Castle is a Victorian-era Scottish baronial mansion that opened
in 1890 (1050 Joan Crescent, www.thecastle.ca).

58 Haunted Loo at The JBI Pub

Peeing is believing

There is only one way to confirm the rumour that the gentlemen's loo at the James Bay Inn Pub, or the JBI, is haunted. You must have a few pints and then go see for yourself.

The backstory on this unusual, unlikely, and yet some say true tale goes back to the 1940s, when in fact there was no pub in the James Bay Inn.

The building was being run as St. Mary's Priory, a wartime convalescence home, and one of its residents was none other than Canadian art icon and lifelong Victoria resident Emily Carr. She was in the final days of her colourful and much-celebrated life, and she passed away in a room that has since been converted into the washroom area of today's James Bay Inn Pub. The hotel is said to be a site of strong paranormal activity, and people have reported a feeling of being watched, phones ringing at odd hours of the night, lights flickering, and so on. Carr's ghost has been reported floating around the gents' and in some of the first-floor bedrooms. Some say she's particularly keen on haunting those who criticise her artwork.

The James Bay Inn Pub is interesting because it is one of those few remarkable places that have stood the test of time. The Inn was built in 1911 on property formerly owned by Bishop Edward Cridge, onetime chaplain at The Hudson's Bay Company in Fort Victoria, and it is the third-oldest hotel in the city. Only the Dominion and The Empress are older, and not by much. One of the Inn's impressive features when it first opened was that all of its one hundred rooms had an outside view. It also had a telephone exchange.

The James Bay area is one of the oldest and best-preserved neighbourhoods, dating back to the earliest days of European settlement, with many architecturally notable buildings still standing nearby.

Address 270 Government Street, Victoria, BC V8V 2L2, +1 (250) 384-7151, www.jamesbayinn.com | Getting there Bus 2, 5, 10 to Menzies at Simcoe | Hours Daily 11am – 10pm | Tip The Carr family home, where Emily was born in 1871, is a two-minute walk away (207 Government Street, www.carrhouse.ca).

59 Helen Stewart's Garden
Unlimited creativity

It's hard to put boundaries on creativity. Painters' and illustrators' ideas can easily exceed the size of their canvases. Writers are often restricted by word counts. Long-time Ten Mile Point resident Helen Stewart knows better than anyone that art should be unrestricted. She is an amazingly prolific artist, writer, teacher, and gardener. Her beautiful, sprawling, one-acre garden, with its rich fertile soil, is alive with the originality in her very special and unique artistic touch. She describes gardening as creating a painting outside.

Stewart was raised and educated in Berkeley, California and also studied at the San Francisco Art Institute and the Art Students League of New York before moving to a farm in Northern British Columbia in 1965. In 1980, the family moved to a large heritage home in Victoria, where she set up her studio and began cultivating and planting the garden that has gone on to become the inspiration for much of her artwork.

You may see the many books she has written and illustrated, along with cards, prints, and calendars inside her home, originally a large old dance hall. It is still used for community events and gatherings, and you can visit it after touring the garden. A lovely, hand-painted flower motif in the hallway leads you to a great room filled with Stewart's prints on the walls and a working press on a big table. A hand-painted sculpture of a life-size pony sits in a corner next to a stylish antique cabinet. The disparate objects in the elegant room all come together naturally, as does her garden outside.

Paul Destrooper, the artistic director of the Ballet Victoria, describes Stewart's imagination as "a magical garden where all plants and creatures find their Eden. Her stories, detailed images, and colours reveal a hidden depth, a reflection of a timeless soul, rich with experience, empathy, love and generosity."

Address 2875 Tudor Avenue, Victoria, BC V8N 1L6, +1 (250) 477-1034, www.hestewart.com, helen@hestewart.com | Getting there Bus 13 to Arbutus at Arbutus Place, then walk 6 minutes | Hours By appointment only | Tip Cadboro-Gyro Park is just down the street from Helen's place. It's a sandy shoreline with logs strewn all over it that also has a beach-themed playground featuring a unique giant octopus slide for the kids (Sinclair Road, www.saanich.ca/EN/main/parks-recreation-community).

60 Helijet Terminal
Be a chopper spotter

Its geography and other economic factors make Victoria a perfect place for a world-class, scheduled helicopter service. Think about it: You have a city of 2.5 million people called Vancouver just across the Salish Sea from another great city of 400,000 people, Victoria. All those people have lots of reasons to go back and forth. They are just over 100km (70 miles) apart as the crow – or the Helijet – flies. The BC Ferry service trip, including driving time, takes over 3 hours. Flying is quicker, but both airports are far from downtown.

With those time-consuming factors in mind, a convenient new service called Helijet was introduced in 1986. Their dynamic president and CEO Danny Sitnam started the company with one single chopper back then. Today, the fleet has grown to over 16. Daily scheduled helicopter services are rare, and Helijet is one of only two in North America.

If you have never watched one of these whirling marvels of aviation land and take off, you should. The Helijet terminal on Dallas Road is the perfect place to do so because you can get quite close to them in their big parking lot, and Helijet has lots of flights arriving and departing daily. There are even picnic tables, so bring your camera, some ear plugs, and a snack, and be prepared to feel the wind stirred up by the helicopters as they gracefully touch down.

A Russian American man named Igor Sikorsky invented the first successful helicopter design as early as 1910. Thirteen of the aircraft in the Helijet fleet today are Sikorsky S-76 helicopters that carry 12 passengers each. The flight between downtown Vancouver and Victoria takes about 15 minutes, and Helijet carries over 100,000 passengers per year. One last thing to consider as you watch these incredible machines descend from the sky less than 100 metres (330 feet) from where you are standing: Helijet has an excellent safety record.

Address 79 Dallas Road, Victoria, BC V8V 15B, +1 (604) 273-4688, www.helijet.com |
Getting there Bus 2, 5 to Dallas at Niagara | **Hours** See website for flight schedule |
Tip Right down the road at the water's edge, the Surf Motel bills itself as Victoria's best
kept secret, and its exterior hasn't changed at all since it was built in 1960 (290 Dallas Road,
www.surfmotel.net).

61 Hermann's Jazz Club
Cool cat central

For over 42 years, mellow notes have emanated from this small, classic Canadian musical institution. Behind the low-profile, drab entrance on View Street, you'll find the longest continually running jazz club in the country. Over the years Hermann's has faced some pretty challenging times, but the consistently amazing music has kept it alive. The jazz club has survived a damaging fire, changes in ownership, a worldwide pandemic, and, most significantly, the death of its colourful founder Hermann Nieweler in 2015 at the age of 79. In the early days, he used to toast with a German rhyme onstage while treating his partying patrons to a round of schnaps on the house. The days of free drinks are gone, and a non-profit entity called the Arts on View Society has taken over management of the Club now.

It's hard to put your finger on what makes the place so special. Its low ceiling, brick walls, subdued lighting, limited number of seats, small stage, rows of long tables, and the world-class acoustics certainly create a cool physical vibe. But it's the musicians who have played there over the years that have kept the place packed and loved by one and all. For a small club, Hermann's only seats 150 people, and it punches above its weight level in terms of attracting internationally acclaimed talent. Wynton Marsalis, Kenny Wheeler, Loudon Wainwright III, Brian Auger, Judy Collins, Eric Bibb, David Francey, and Rob McConnell have all played here.

Vancouver Island is a hotbed of musical talent, and just as importantly, all its great local jazz bands continue to grace the stage at Hermann's, including CanUS, The Dixieland Express, the Tom Vickery Trio, and local legendary saxophone and clarinet player Al Pease. One thing is for certain: When you visit the club, Hermann Nieweler's love for a lively, rollicking party, great music, tasty food, and happy guests lives on.

Address 753 View Street, Victoria, BC V8W 1J9, +1 (250) 388-9166, www.hermannsjazz.com, info@hermannsjazz.com | Getting there Bus 3, 6, 11, 14, 22 to Fort at Blanshard | Hours See website for schedule and events | Tip Another Victoria musical institution is the Royal Victoria Theatre, which opened in 1913 and is home to the Victoria Symphony Orchestra. In 1987, it was declared a National Historic Site and is worth checking out for the building's design and architecture (805 Broughton Street, www.rmts.bc.ca/theatres/royal-theatre).

62 — The Home of Spoony Singh

The moderne marvel of a Hollywood icon

You've probably heard of the Hollywood Wax Museum in Los Angeles and the Guinness World Records Museum just across the street. Both museums are the creative and entrepreneurial output of Sapuran "Spoony" Singh, who built this home – an incredible example of moderne architecture – for himself and wife Chanchil Kour Hoti in 1954.

Though Spoony is perhaps best remembered for his Hollywood days, it was here in Victoria where his dreams first took root. The house is "moderne" because it has the features typical of that architectural style: a flat roof and windows with a horizontal emphasis. It's close to the "streamline moderne" style that was popular in the 1930s, often seen on iconic CP Rail travel posters of that era, and various chrome-clad American roadside Diners and beachfront Miami Hotels with pink Cadillacs parked in front. Spoony was a modern character, and he built a moderne house full of it.

Spoony came to Victoria from Punjab, made enough money in lumber mills and camps to build this house, and opened an amusement park in Esquimalt called "Spoony's," featuring home-made, chainsaw-powered go-karts. With more success came bigger dreams, and Spoony moved to Hollywood in the mid-1960s. His big personality resonated, and he became an even bigger success there – he was known for riding an elephant in the local parades. He even branched out to open a wax museum in Missouri featuring a faux Mount Rushmore with the heads of John Wayne, Elvis Presley, Marilyn Monroe, and Charlie Chaplin.

When he died in his Malibu home in 2006, Spoony made news one final time with obituaries in the *Los Angeles Times*, *The New York Times*, the *Toronto Globe and Mail* and many others. You can see where he lived before he became Mr. Hollywood, but there's no parking for elephants.

Address 3210 Bellevue Road, Victoria, BC V8X 1C1 | Getting there Bus 25 to Maplewood at Ocean View | Hours Unrestricted from the outside only | Tip The Dr. H. Johns House is another well-preserved moderne house, designed in 1938 (2753 Somass Drive, www.historicplaces.ca).

63__The Human Sundial
Telling time, the hard way

This unique 18-foot-wide sundial commemorates the province of British Columbia's 150th anniversary, celebrated in 2008. It was a collaboration between local activist Andrei Golovkine, who came up with the concept, and Dr. Dmitry Monin, an astrophysicist at the National Research Council's Herzberg Institute. It is incredibly impractical and confusing for those who are best suited to things like writing guidebooks or drawing pictures, but if you're into maths and astrophysics, you'll be intrigued.

This sundial is known by experts as an analemmatic sundial, which means that it uses a human as its gnomon, the piece in the middle of a sundial that casts a shadow used to tell the hour. But you don't just stand in the middle of this sundial and cast a shadow. No, that would be too easy. Because it's an analemmatic sundial, you have to stand at varying locations on a scale, dictated by the current date, to cast the necessary shadow on brass Roman numerals displayed around the rim.

Walk onto the dial, look down at the scale, and read the various adjustment factors you can make at different times of the year to get an accurate result. Be sure to come on a sunny day so that you'll cast your shadow. It has been known to be foggy in Victoria, and when that happens, there's no amount of maths you can do to make the sundial work.

Regardless of your affinity for overly complicated time-telling devices, the sundial is worth seeing because it's a fascinating and historical instrument. It's weirdly interesting and located in an area with a great view of the ocean. On a clear day, you can not only tell the time, but you can also see the United States. Plus, you never know when the winning, million-dollar question on a game show or your local pub's trivia night will be something like, "What is an analemmatic sundial?" Or "What is the thing in the middle of a sundial called?"

Address 211 Dallas Road, Victoria, BC V8V 1B1 | **Getting there** Bus 2, 5 to Dallas at Montreal |
Hours Unrestricted | **Tip** The Dallas Road Staircase is a short, pleasant walk along the beach
and will reward you with a colourful and mysterious experience (Dallas Road & San Jose Avenue).

64_ The Island Circus Space
Put yourself through the hoops

There's no clowning around at this circus, though they do have a lot of fun. Victoria's first contemporary circus school is part of the hidden Victoria you don't often hear about, and its off-the-beaten-path, semi-industrial location keeps it out of mainstream attention. But you might want to hang out here.

Circus performers Coral Crawford and Lisa Eckert created the Island Circus Space in 2016 after spending years teaching and learning on their own at different places across Canada and abroad. Today, there are over a dozen instructors associated with the Circus Space, all with similar credentials and an unswerving addiction to this creative routine, which combines elements of ballet, yoga, gymnastics, and performance art.

Located in a former produce warehouse, the unassuming Rock Bay studio space has padded floors and custom-built steel beams with special pulleys and rigging engineered to create a safe environment for all who aspire to do their bendy exercises off the ground. If you're more of an on-the-ground person, you can also do partner aerobics and flexibility training here.

It doesn't matter if you're 14 or 40, beginner or expert, the space – replete with hanging ropes of silk – has everything you need to get in on the act. The skilled instructors will help you learn the aerial hoop and trapeze, handstands, hammock silks, silks and rope, and aerial straps. The trainers will also guide you along a creative process that allows you to channel your newfound physical skills into a performance of your own design, as every class ends with an opportunity for practitioners to perform at a "student cabaret." If the idea of repeatedly lifting weights up and down or bicycling to nowhere on a machine seems boring to you, and you'd rather get fit while doing something creative, maybe it's time to run away and join the Island Circus Space.

Address 3–625 Hillside Avenue, Victoria, BC V8T 1Z1, +1 (250) 532-8282, www.islandcircusspace.com | Getting there Bus 9, 11 to Gorge at Government at Douglas | Hours See website for class schedules | Tip Parachute Ice Cream a block away is a favourite location for circus performers to chill out and unwind (105–2626 Bridge Street, www.parachuteicecream.com).

65 John's Place

Where the home plate is stacked with pancakes

John Cantin, a young and adventurous chef, thought it would be fun to drive from Los Angeles to Victoria in his classic 1967 Volkswagen van. He didn't plan on staying long – he was going to trek around Tahiti – but when he saw a boarded-up old fish-and-chips restaurant on Pandora Street, he was "hooked." Renovations and much toil later, John's Place opened in October 1984 and is now known as one of the best spots in town for a hearty breakfast. And if you're a baseball fan, so much the better, as the walls are covered in nostalgic photos of the great players and teams.

Over the years, the restaurant and its walls have become famous. The baseball pictures have been supplemented with images from other sports, and those have been supplemented with images from all kinds of entertainers and celebrities. Look around, and you'll see autographs from diners like major league baseball player Joe Carter, Canadian music legends the Barenaked Ladies and Ron Sexsmith. Canadian artists Nelly Furtado and Sarah McLachlan have also tucked into a hearty breakfast here. Noted British actor Chiwitel Ejiofor has been here, as has late American actress Kirstie Alley.

You'll be gazing around at the walls while you're supposed to be looking at the menu, but when you do look down, you'll find hearty, wholesome diner-style offerings from traditional bacon and eggs to "Bat out of hell meatloaf and eggs," and a variety of waffles, pancakes, and more. Breakfast is served all day, but if you like soup for lunch, ask about the bottomless bowl.

John is still a regular sight at John's Place but the next generation is increasingly present – that young man welcoming you just might be his son Norm. In any case, whenever you visit, you're guaranteed to be treated like family, amazed by the sport-and-star-spangled walls, and leave with a happy and full stomach. Batter up – you're next!

Address 723 Pandora Avenue, Victoria, BC V8W 1N9, +1 (250) 389-0711, www.johnsplace.ca, info@johnsplace.ca | Getting there Bus 4, 30, 31, 32, 44, 47, 48, 53, 61, 65, 66, 70, 71, 72, 75, 95, 99 to Douglas at Pandora | Hours Daily 8am – 3pm | Tip Down the street, check out the shops in the Maynard Building. This structure was built around 1890 and, as home to Grimm's Carriage Works, it used to have a full-size carriage suspended over the front door (733 Pandora Street).

66 Johnson Street Bridge
Why didn't they paint it blue?

For a city surrounded by the ocean, harbours, and inlets Victoria doesn't have many bridges. The most famous iconic one, the Johnson Street Bridge, is in the middle of town. It's a beautiful, modern, sleek-looking bridge that is noteworthy for a number of reasons. First of all, its colour. Painting it white was a questionable decision. The bridge that it replaced was an old beauty built in 1924. Residents loved it, and for decades they fondly referred to it as the Blue Bridge. It was not only a historic landmark, but a real reference point for directions. If you were trying to give someone directions to a particular place downtown, you'd often start with its location in relation to the Blue Bridge.

So, it's a good thing that the new bridge, erected in 2018, is so unique looking and still stands out. Part of that is due to its futuristic design with its geometric tapered truss sections. Like the old blue bridge, this new white one is a bascule bridge, also referred to as a drawbridge or lifting bridge. It has a balanced counterweight, a hydraulic motor, and gears that make it possible to lift part of the road up to provide clearance for the boat traffic below. This style of bridge dates back to the mediaeval era, when smaller scale versions of them were built as the entrances to castles and towers surrounded by deep and foreboding moats.

Other great modern features of this new bridge include three traffic lanes, a wide pedestrian walkway on its south side, and a multi-use pathway on its other side. The bridge's bright night lighting was even designed so as not to disturb the sea life below. The new Johnson Street Bridge is Canada's longest single-leaf bascule bridge. You may be asking yourself, what is the charge for them to lift the massive, several-ton span if your boat is too tall to sneak underneath? That's easy: $75.00, and 90-minutes' notice is required.

Address 400 Johnson Street, Victoria, BC V8W 0B2 | Getting there Bus 14, 15, 24, 25 to Pandora at Government/Store | Hours Unrestricted | Tip At the east end of the bridge is *Commerce Canoe* by artist Illarion Gallant, one of Victoria's most interesting civic art installations. It's a big, sparkling aluminium canoe cradled in the centre of 7 36-foot-tall, bright red seed pod reeds (1226 Commercial Alley, www.crd.bc.ca).

67 — The Kiwanis Tea Room at Willow Beach

Spectacular view with a $15 Breakfast

People in North America just don't volunteer as much as they used to. Community service organisations like the Kiwanis, Rotary, and Lions clubs are having a tough time attracting new members and young people. The average age of the local Oak Bay Kiwanis Club is 70-years old. Just before most of those members were born, the local Kiwanis club took on an ambitious project at the time, organising an important fundraising initiative and location that has lasted to this day.

They built a teahouse on the beach in 1947 and started selling hot dogs, tea, and coffee. The Kiwanis Tea Room instantly became a philanthropic success, and the next year the club raised over $700, which it donated to local youth recreational projects. Today, they are still going strong, raising tens of thousands of dollars a year for charity. The teahouse is as popular as ever.

The view from the tearoom is the real draw. The beachfront location has one of the nicest unobstructed vistas in Victoria, and the food and hot drinks are cheaper than what you would pay at some of the fancier establishments up the beach. The building is about as far from pretentious as you can get and is actually a pretty austere facility, but its history and sense of community purpose complement the breathtaking scenery.

The 29-seat restaurant is normally open in the spring and summer and offers $15.00 breakfasts on Sundays between 9am and noon. That's where you can witness firsthand some of the old-fashioned community spirit for which the Kiwanis are famous. The food is made and served by a group of six volunteers. The first weekend of June is a great time to visit the Kiwanis Willow Beach Tea Room for the annual Oak Bay Tea Party. It attracts thousands of people and begins with a big parade to kick it off.

Address 2740 Dalhousie Road, Victoria, BC V8R 2J1, +1 (250) 592-1612, www.oakbaytourism.com/ stakeholder/willows-tea-room | Getting there Bus 5 to Beach at Dalhousie | Hours See website for seasonal hours | Tip A short, pleasant stroll from the Tea Room is Tod House, the home of John Tod, Hudson's Bay Company's chief fur trader and one of the first appointed members of BC's Legislative Council (2564 Heron Street, www.oakbay.ca/explore-oak-bay/points-interest/tod-house).

68 Lego Hotel
Lego in the lobby

We all had a bit of down time on our hands during the pandemic to catch up on our hobbies. Chateau Victoria bellman Glen Waddingham took his spare time to an extreme and built something worth seeing. He clearly loves his job; he loves the building he works in – and he loves Lego. He has a collection of 62,000 Lego pieces, to be exact. What was once boxes and boxes overflowing with the colourful plastic, square and rectangular toy building blocks is now a beautiful replica of Chateau Victoria, the city's most iconic downtown hotel. During those two long pandemic years, he constructed a one-of-a-kind, miniature version of this Burdett Avenue landmark.

The tiny details he built into his model are amazing. Having spent 30 years working there, Waddingham was very familiar with the hotel's roof lines, all the interior and exterior walls, and every nook and cranny of the 177-guest-room hotel. But it's not only the architectural features that make this model so special. Take the time to check out the miniature people walking around outside, look for the tiny guy cleaning the windows while dangling off of a rope, and spot a co-worker carrying her supersized drink in hand. If you look hard enough, you will even see someone making a marriage proposal, gold ring and all.

The Lego model is a quirky thing to have in a hotel lobby. But peer into suite 1602 for a quirky fact to look for in the model itself. That's where you will see Waddingham's birth parents (he was adopted) enjoying the view. After being reunited with them in 1991, he invited them to stay in the hotel in the actual suite 1602, the best room in the property. Look for the tiny replicas of them relaxing on that room's balcony. Lego Hotel is a wonderfully personal project done with passion and pride.

Address 740 Burdett Avenue, Victoria, BC V8W 1B2, +1 (250) 382-4221, https://chateauvictoria.com | Getting there Bus 27, 28 to Fairfield at Blanchard, or bus 4, 7, 27, 28 to Burdett at Douglas | Hours Unrestricted during lobby hours | Tip Just a few blocks away is Thunderbird Park, established in 1941, featuring an interesting display of totem poles. The park is named for the mythological Thunderbird, which is featured on many of the totem poles (638 Douglas Street, www.tourismvictoria.com).

69　Lochside Trail Pigs
Pigs de resistance

To the untrained eye, pigs just lie in mud between 18 and 20 hours a day, not doing much. The two very laid-back ones that live just off the busy Lochside Trail are no exception, especially when compared to the fit, active people passing by.

The trail attracts joggers, walkers, cyclists, and others pursuing fresh air, amazing views, interesting stops, and a safe, pristine environment for exercise. These pigs do indeed mainly sleep, eat, and get up occasionally to greet visitors. They've been here for years, joyfully relaxing under a crude, wooden shelter with half a dozen old tires on top preventing the plywood roof from flying off. These pigs are retired and have a carefree life because they have no obligation to breed or fears of becoming bacon. According to their owner Frans, their job is simply to just hang out along the Lochside Trail and make people happy. And he ought to know: he has kept pigs here for over 50 years.

If they look kind of fat to you, that is because they are well fed. There are always boxes and boxes of slightly dated vegetables lying next to them on the other side of the fence. Passers-by can easily bend over, pick up an onion or carrot, and try to lure one of them out of their hut. They have real personalities, too, and they've started to attract regular visitors and a bit of media attention.

Contrary to popular belief, pigs are actually very social and intelligent animals. These pigs even have their own social media account. Check out @lochsidepigs on Instagram for some great pictures of them and other animals on the farm. They are not camera shy, so why not take a selfie with them behind the fence before you get moving again on the trail? As you depart, you can reflect on a famous quote about pigs from none other than Sir Winston Churchill, who once said, "I am fond of pigs. Dogs look up to us. Cats look down on us. Pigs treat us as equals."

Address 6500 Lochside Drive, Saanichton, BC V8M 1Y2, www.instagram.com/lochsidepigs | Getting there Bus 75 to Tanner at Marie Meadows | Hours Unrestricted | Tip Just north of the pigs' hut, you'll find Whale Tail Farms. You can't miss its multiple giant, rusty, metal whale tails poking out of a field next to the side of the road (6600 Lochside Trail, Saanichton, www.instagram.com/whale.tail.farm).

70 Macdonald's Last Stand

Unceremoniously dumped

Here stood Sir John A. Macdonald, first Prime Minister of Canada. At least, here stood his statue from the date it was first installed on July 1, 1982, until it was unceremoniously removed on August 11, 2018. The work, created by sculptor John Dann, had been commissioned by the Sir John A. Macdonald Historical Society and presented to the City of Victoria to commemorate Macdonald as a founder of Canada and member of Parliament for the city. The installation was a grand public event, as Lt. Governor Henry Irving-Bell unveiled the statue in the presence of the artist, with Victoria Mayor Peter Pollen and several other dignitaries looking on.

If the presentation of the statue was public and dignified, its removal was anything but. Without any public consultation or forewarning, on the evening of August 9, 2018, City Council passed a motion to remove it and – in a remarkable demonstration of rarely seen municipal efficiency – had it wrapped in foam, hoisted onto a flatbed truck, and spirited out of sight in less than 48 hours. The $30,000 cost to remove it was also approved with startling speed. By the time word of the decision had leaked out, there was nothing that could be done to stop it. About one hundred citizens showed up on Saturday morning to witness the removal, some cheering, and some protesting in equal measure, but there was nothing to do but watch as the removal order was executed.

Macdonald's disappearing act may have seemed hasty and undemocratic, yet it was a more dignified affair than the later removal of Victoria's Captain Cook statue. That statue had decorated the Inner Harbour since 1976, but, gripped by the statue-toppling fever of 2022, activists tossed it into the harbour. Not having the benefit of foam wrapping, it was too damaged to be reinstalled. As for the Macdonald statue, it has been quietly escorted off the Island.

Address 1 Centennial Square, Victoria, BC V8W 1P6 | **Getting there** Bus 4, 11, 21, 22, 30, 31, 32, 47, 48, 53, 61, 65, 70, 71, 72, 75, 95 to Douglas at Pandora/City Hall | **Hours** Unrestricted | **Tip** Centennial Square's central fountain is surrounded by a white balustrade and contains three massive, modern monoliths made from over 500,000 pieces of Italian glass. The work by artist Jack Wilkinson was gifted to the city by neighbouring municipalities to mark its centennial in 1962 (1 Centennial Square, www.crd.bc.ca/landmarks/artworks).

71__ The Malahat Skywalk
Ramp up and slide down

Malahat Skywalk not only offers great views, but it is also interesting to look at. From the top of the Skywalk, some 250 metres (829 feet) above sea level, the tower gives you a sweeping view of the Saanich Inlet, Finlayson Arm, Mt. Baker – in the distance on a clear day – and various islands in Canada and the US. And the architecture of the Skywalk is itself something to behold.

Built from wood and steel, at a cost of some seventeen million dollars, the Skywalk looks a bit like a giant waffle cone. You get to it by strolling through the TreeWalk, a peaceful forest of arbutus and Douglas fir trees, and then around an increasingly upward and gently spiralling walkway that takes you to the top. Once there, if you're bold enough, you can crawl out onto the Adventure Net and look straight down through the actual net to see how far you've come (32 metres/105 feet). After taking in the views, you have a few options on how to get back to earth: down the Skywalk ramp, down the spiral staircase in the middle, or, if you're looking for some thrills, down the Spiral Slide, which wraps around the staircase.

Another feature of the Skywalk is that it is located on the traditional and ancestral territory of the Malahat Nation, and their Indigenous culture is embedded in the natural environment and visitor experience. The eco-art installations by Tanya Bub of various animals made from tree roots really make the connection to the land in a fun way. On the tower itself, you'll find panels that point out unique characteristics of local flora and fauna. Panels at the top highlight local birds and environmental factors that impact the region. There's also information on topics such as moon cycles and sea life that blends Indigenous knowledge and Western science. The Welcome Centre is a source for some indigenous artwork, jewellery, textiles and carvings.

Address 901 Trans-Canada Highway, Malahat, BC V0R 2L0, +1 (833) 625-2428, www.malahatskywalk.com, info@malahatskywalk.com | Getting there By car, northbound on the Trans-Canada Highway, take the exit approximately 800 metres past the Malahat Summit Viewpoint, and park at the Malahat Skywalk parking lot. From downtown Victoria, Island Time Tours (+1 (250) 477-3322) offers a daily shuttle service with pick up from four convenient locations. | Hours See website for seasonal hours | Tip The Split Rock Viewpoint offers a stunning view across the Saanich Inlet toward Brentwood Bay and Butchart Gardens (2.16 kilometres (1.3 miles) after re-entering the Trans-Canada Highway from the Malahat Skywalk turnoff).

72 Mammoth Driftwood Sculpture

Bones near the beach

Victoria has no shortage of craggy, salty, errant driftwood logs. Most people strolling along the dozens of beaches here probably pass the water-soaked logs without giving them much thought, not realising that they are an ideal artistic medium. Local artist Alex Witcomb, however, sees each log as a beautiful, unique element in the sculptures he creates on Vancouver Island.

You can find a remarkable example of Witcomb's art, with an interesting prehistoric local footnote, near Colwood's Royal Beach Playground Park. Look for a life-sized sculpture of a giant, elephant-like creature known as a mammoth, along with a smaller baby mammoth. Witcomb created them both entirely out of driftwood he found on the beach near where they stand.

And why mammoths? About a kilometre away, up the hill, in the direction the mammoths are looking, is a new housing development called Royal Bay. For 112 years, the land on which all those new houses and stores are being built was a large gravel pit. While workers were excavating it back in the 1960s, they found a tooth from one of these extinct giants. Archeologists figure that the ancient molar is about 18,000 years old. That makes sense because the species roamed the cold tundra of North America from about 300,000 years ago to as recently as 4,000 years ago. The last ones to die out lived on remote islands, including, we now know, Vancouver Island.

Whitcomb is an amazing artist who lives in the Comox Valley on Vancouver Island. Aside from creating driftwood sculptures, he also paints murals, writes and illustrates children's books, and draws and creates digital illustrations. The next time you're near Campbell River, look for a large dinosaur sculpture, also made of driftwood on Stories Beach.

Address 3483 Metchosin Road, Victoria, BC V9C 1Z1, +1 (250) 792-4226, www.driftedcreationsart.ca, alexwitcombe@gmail.com | Getting there Bus 52, 54, 59 to Latoria at Dunlin | Hours Unrestricted | Tip If mammoths interest you, then go see the most photographed life-size replica of one in the entire world at The Royal Victoria Museum. The signature replica piece here is very furry and very realistic (675 Belleville Street, www.royalbcmuseum.bc.ca).

73 Mille Fleurs
Mysterious royal hideaway

"Royal watchers" will remember that there was a time when Prince Harry and Meghan Markle were hiding out somewhere on the coast of British Columbia.

It was Christmastime 2019 when the two recently-weds first came to a mansion called Mille Fleurs. Music giant David Foster had helped hook them up with this hideaway not too far from his childhood home. By January 2020, mellowed perhaps by the serenity of the location, they announced that they were going to step back as senior members of the British royal family. Putting some physical distance between themselves and the establishment was a key part of the plan.

Surrounded by two beaches, landscaped gardens, and Canadian neighbours who know how to mind their own business, Mille Fleurs was the perfect, post-regal getaway. Yet Harry, Meghan, and baby Archie only stayed in the 1,200-square-metre (13,000 square-foot) main house for about six months. By the summer of 2020, the travel-banning COVID pandemic threatened to keep them here longer than they had planned. So, they rolled up their red carpets and moved to California.

People often wonder who owns the mystery mansion. It's complicated. According to the CBC and other sources, it's actually part of a corporation associated with a company in the British Virgin Islands, whose management is owned by another company registered in the Bahamas, which is owned by a trust in Jersey, whose sole officer lives in Cyprus. The venture capitalist Yuri Milner has many ties with the entertainment crowd, including David Foster. But even though most common folk would be proud to claim ownership of such a regal retreat, the billionaire class seem either not to know what they own or have been told by their accountants and lawyers to keep their traps shut. So, who owns the joint? Who knows. But if you know the right people, you might just be able to get the keys.

Address 525 Towner Road, North Saanich, BC V8L 5L8 | Getting there Bus 85 to Downey at Madrona | Hours Unrestricted from the outside only | Tip Due to security concerns, Deep Cove Chalet famously declined a reservation request from Harry and Meghan, but if you call in advance you might be able to enjoy the fine French cuisine and ocean views (11190 Chalet Road, North Saanich, www.deepcovechalet.com).

74 Miniature World
Honey, I shrunk the attraction

The City of Victoria holds the record for hosting the world's smallest display at Miniature World. At the same time, the display also provides a big educational insight into the most important industry on Vancouver Island, which is logging.

Someone actually took the time to build the world's smallest, fully operational sawmill. That person was Phil Quelch, and he called it the "Little Mills Lumber Company." And equally impressive as the miniature sawmill itself is the fact that Quelch spent 11 years constructing it. That's an astonishing amount of time, especially when you consider that there are dozens of massive, real-life sawmills up and down the coast of Vancouver Island that were built in less than a few years. See if you can spot the tiny circular gang saw.

In addition to the extraordinarily detailed sawmill, there are 84 other miniature dioramas on display at the museum, some of them "near" record holders. They include one of the world's largest miniature dollhouses, an enticing oxymoron to be sure. The Great Canadian Railway Experience, one of the world's largest model railways is worth a very close look. Pay attention to all of the tiny features, right down to the train's smokestacks and ornate dining cars. Look for a colourful circus, complete with a Grand City Parade, the Big Top, wild animals, and a high-wire act. The display with the changing of the guards at Buckingham Palace is delightful too, as is the Enchanted Valley of Castles.

In a world full of high-tech museum presentations, big video screens, and elaborate interactive and interpretative stations, it is refreshing to visit the simple, old fashioned, wooden display cases at Miniature World. They haven't changed much since it first opened in 1971. And while it's a bit touristy, there's something here for locals to enjoy on occasional visits to Victoria's own small tourist district.

Address 649 Humboldt Street, Victoria, BC V8W 1A7, +1 (250) 384-2847, www.visitorinvictoria.ca/miniature-world-victoria-bc, visitorinvictoria@gmail.com | Getting there Bus 1, 2, 3, 5, 27, 28, 30, 31, 32, 44, 48, 53, 61, 65, 66, 70, 71, 72, 75, 95, 99 to Douglas at Humboldt | Hours Daily, see website for seasonal hours | Tip Just around the corner from Miniature World is the Maritime Museum of BC, with over 800 models of ships and other items related to the province's marine heritage (744 Douglas Street, www.mmbc.bc.ca).

75 __ The Moss Lady
Lay, lady, lay

There is no big brass bed for this lady to lay on, just a big grass bed. And what a beautiful and serene vision she is – surely enough to inspire your inner Bob Dylan to compose a line or two of poetry.

You can find this 11-metre-long (36-foot) art piece on the west side of Beacon Hill Park, between Douglas Street and the Cameron Bandshell, just south of Goodacre Lake. Conceived and created by gardener Dale Doebert, with help from Victoria City employees, the work depicts a moss-covered woman partly submerged in the earth. Installed in 2015, it is one of only a few in the world. The inspiration for this one is *The Mud Maid*, located in The Lost Gardens of Heligan in Cornwall, England. There's another green gal at Waterfall Cottage in Sydney, Australia called *Lily*.

Victoria's *Moss Lady* is green but not entirely organic: her structure is made from cement, boulders, metal pipe, and vinyl-coated chicken wire. The next layer is clay-based soil and locally sourced cattail and club moss to fill out the rest; the lady's "hair" is made from flowering crocosmia plants. The park she rests in was created in 1882, when the Province of British Columbia granted the land to the City of Victoria in trust.

The ginormous, 74 hectares (183 acres) of nature offer lots to see and do besides visiting *The Moss Lady*. The park has two playgrounds, a golf putting green, baseball diamond, cricket pitch, tennis courts, lawn bowling, footpaths, a rose garden, and even a Children's Farm. Kite enthusiasts, paragliders, and sailboarders enjoy the open vista across the Strait of Juan De Fuca. Ecologically speaking, the most notable feature in the park is its extensive, natural Garry oak ecosystem. Geographically speaking, the park is notable because it includes Mile "0" of the 8,000 kilometre-long Trans-Canada Highway. *The Moss Lady* is a little tricky to find, but that's part of the fun.

Address Beacon Hill Park, across from 250 Douglas Street, Victoria, BC V8V 2P4, www.victoria.ca/EN/main/residents/parks/beacon-hill.html | **Getting there** Bus 2, 5, 10 to Douglas at Avalon | **Hours** Unrestricted | **Tip** Just south of *The Moss Lady* is a pagoda-style structure that marks the spot where the "Boxer Bell of Beacon Hill Park" used to be. The ancient relic from the Boxer Rebellion is now in the Victoria Art Gallery, but it hung here from 1904–1989 (1040 Moss Street, www.aggv.ca).

76 Mount Tolmie Tales
Views, vistas, trails, and toboggans

Everyone knows that some of the best views of Victoria are had from the top of Mount Tolmie. You can see downtown Victoria, Beacon Hill Park, the Strait of Juan de Fuca, the Saanich area, Gordon Head, and the University of Victoria from here.

But there's more to this mountain than awesome views. The strangest story – evidence of which is long gone except for what's in the newspaper archives – is that it was home to what may have been Canada's first amusement park.

It was on Mount Tolmie, in 1891, that the 16-acre park was home to a snowless toboggan slide that *The BC Colonist* described as being "perfect in every particular, and only differing from the favourite pastime of Eastern Canada in its not being dependent on snow for its running powers." The slide was 140 metres (460 feet) long, and the toboggans, which were 1.8 metres (6 feet) long and .6 metres (2 feet) wide, fit into square grooves that guided their descent. At the end of the ride, the toboggans were hauled back to the top by cables. Sadly, the slide burned down a few years later, and leaving little trace.

Another long-gone story is the time during World War II, when the military stationed observers at the top of Tolmie. An additional easy-to-overlook feature of Tolmie is its water reservoir. If you ever wondered why the nearby sports field is so perfectly flat, it's because it is the grass-covered roof of the 4.8-million-litre water reservoir that provides drinking water to the residents of Victoria.

The present-day use of Tolmie as a viewing and picnic area began in the 1950s. Since the 1990s, the Mount Tolmie Conservation Association has been working to revive and improve the Mount's forty-five acres of parkland, and now you can enjoy more than 1.5 kilometres (1 mile) of trails, along with picnic areas and plenty of prime spots to watch some of the estimated 100 species of birds that favour the slopes.

Address Mount Tolmie, Victoria, BC V8P 49P, www.victoriatrails.com/trails/mount-tolmie | Getting there Bus 14 to Richmond at Mayfair, then walk 11 minutes up Mayfair | Hours Unrestricted | Tip Aquatic amusements can be found for kids at the nearby Oak Bay Rotary Water Park in Carnarvon Park (2801 Henderson Road, www.visitorinvictoria.ca/carnavon-park-victoria-bc).

77 Musical Railings
Keep the beat at Bastion Square Parkade

They may have paved paradise to put up a parking lot, as the song goes, but at least this lot has a musical staircase. Artists Scott Amos and David Parfit have created a totally unique, light-sensitive handrail that plays a beat, sound, or musical note when you grip it. This hands-on public art will put a spring in your step.

Amos, a filmmaker and media artist, whose business card identifies him as a "Mostly Harmless Mad Scientist," and Parfit, an established music composer for film and television and something of a computer wizard, have programmed the handrail with sounds that can be modified to correspond with seasonal themes, such as bird song in the spring, jazz samples or chords during JazzFest in the summer, or the sound of jingle bells during the holidays. Not only can the type and variety of sounds be changed, but the installation can also be reconfigured to showcase different musicians, composers and poets.

Just as there are different strokes for different folks, these railings can accommodate different sounds for each flight of stairs. The railings are programmed with audio content, and they are also programmed to display stimulating visual content. This is the one instance when a nighttime visit to a parking lot staircase is a fun idea. And that's kind of the point of this artwork: to turn scary parking lots into a place of joy and whimsy, and to turn a mundane task into a pleasurable activity. The mad scientist and the inspired composer have converted what was formerly a utilitarian and unattractive piece of infrastructure into a carnival of sight and sound.

The two artists have had their works displayed in a number of places and festivals, such as the Art Gallery of Greater Victoria, the Victoria Film Festival, Bass Coast Music and Arts Festival. But this is one installation you have to come and see for yourself. Parking won't be a problem.

Address 575 Yates Street, Victoria, BC V8W 2Z6, www.monkeycinteractive.com/#/musicalrailings | Getting there Bus 14, 15 to Wharf at Yates | Hours Unrestricted | Tip Refresh yourself with tea from Murchie's, a block away and founded by a Scotsman who used to deliver tea to Queen Victoria at Balmoral Castle in 1894 (1110 Government Street, www.murchies.com).

78 — Ogden Point Breakwater
Home to Canada's longest mural

At first sight, it may look unremarkable, but the Ogden Point Breakwater is quite fascinating. It's a great place to go for a walk along an easy, 1.5-kilometre (1-mile) round trip that only takes half an hour and offers all the fresh air you can breathe.

When you reach the lighthouse, you'll have a beautiful view south toward the Juan de Fuca Strait, west to Macaulay Point Park in Esquimalt, and north towards the James Bay area. If your timing is right, you might see helicopters and float planes coming in for landings. But stop for a moment and contemplate what's under your feet because what you've been walking on is an incredible feat of engineering. In fact, the breakwater was named a National Historic Civil Engineering Site in 2001. That's because the 762-metre (.5-mile), granite and concrete wall is made from over 1,000,000 cubic yards of locally quarried rock and 10,000 granite blocks weighing up to 15 tons each. It's been virtually maintenance-free since completion in 1916.

You're also standing on a very important part of Victoria's history. Its origins date back to 1883, when R. P. Rithet trailblazed the development of wharves that could handle the deep-sea trade ships that were too big to enter the inner harbour. When the Panama Canal opened in 1914, even more trade to Victoria was imminent, and a million dollars was allocated to building the Ogden Breakwater. Two years later, it was open for business. In today's dollars, the cost would be a billion dollars, and it would take as many years just to do the paperwork.

Finally, if you look at the inner side of the breakwater, you'll notice it's covered in art. This is *The Unity Wall*, sponsored by the Greater Victoria Harbour Authority to honour the long tradition and rich history of the South Salish Esquimalt and Songhees Nations in the area. It is also Canada's longest mural.

Address 211 Dallas Road, Victoria, BC V6V 1A1, www.victoriatrails.com/trails/ogden-point-breakwater | Getting there Bus 2, 5 to Dallas at Montreal | Hours Unrestricted | Tip One of Victoria's oldest homes, built in 1879 for Mrs. Anne Cox, is just a few steps away (152 Dallas Road).

79_The Original Jam Cafe

Hash browns and heritage on Herald Street

There are three Jam Cafes in British Columbia, but the original one, the one that got it all started, is this one on Herald Street. Opened in 2012 and constantly challenged with line-ups of customers craving their menu of hearty Canadian comfort foods, Jam's owners opened another location on Vancouver's Beatty Street in 2016 and then followed up with their Kitsilano location in 2018. So, if you want to see and taste what got the jam rolling, you really must come here to find out.

Normally, when you think about a café, you think about food. But what Jam really has is a certain unique style. An ethos. It's one of those things that's hard to describe, but you know it when you see it – or taste it. Maybe it's "Rustic Canadian," or maybe it's "Urban Retro." In any case, while they do serve takeout, this is one of those eateries where the place itself makes the food taste better – being here is half the experience.

When you enter, you'll find an intimate, cosy space as warm as a Hudson's Bay blanket. Look toward the bar and take in the antique National Cash Register and, for no good reason at all, a bowling pin. Elsewhere on a shelf, there's an old radio from the 1950s. On the walls are a few felt pennants – the kind those of the Boomer generation collected on road trips – and a stuffed, mounted, elk head. Bright red subway tiles complement the white ceramic coffee mugs that bring you your first tasting experience. Now comes the food. The Fat Elvis waffle combines bananas, peanut butter, and bacon in a way that would make The King proud. The Smashed Avocado Benny makes avocado toast blush.

The Jam Cafe is a great place with a hearty, almost nostalgic menu that fits well with the café's location within one of three storefronts of the Herald Building, a three-story, brick structure built in 1913 for local entrepreneurs Lim Bang and Wong Jan Way.

Address 542 Herald Street, Victoria, BC V8W 1S6, +1 (778) 440-4489, www.jamcafes.com, jamcafe@shaw.ca | **Getting there** Bus 4, 11, 21, 22, 30, 31, 32, 47, 48, 53, 61, 65, 70, 71, 72, 75 to Douglas at Herald/Fisgard | **Hours** Mon–Fri 8am–2pm, Sat & Sun 8am–3pm | **Tip** Look for the nearby mural *Lady Justice* by artist Steve Milroy, who designed it to honour the Victoria Integrated Court (VIC) initiative (533 Chatham Street).

80 The Painted Poles of Fernwood

A small community initiative that went global

Victoria's Fernwood District has the most beautiful painted street poles. This colourful community art project to encourage residents to apply old, discarded paint with artistic flair to round wooden power poles, even caught the eye of dozens of national and international media outlets, including *The New York Times*. All of that media attention resulted in cities around the world replicating and expanding the successful project. Now there are painted polls in places from Honduras to Japan that can trace their initiatives to the little Victoria neighbourhood of Fernwood. The US alone has several cities that credit Fernwood for planting the poll-painting seed. In 2014, a group from Springfield, Missouri visited to learn how to implement their own project.

British Columbia has about 900,000 wooden power poles, including 500 in this leafy neighbourhood. Up until 2008, Fernwood's poles were drab, dull, grey, and utilitarian – until local resident and artist Beth Threlfall stepped in with her paintbrush and collaborative vision. At first, she just painted the pole in front of her house, and the feed-back she received was amazingly positive. Then she encouraged others in the neighbourhood to begin painting poles too.

The eco-friendly program even uses paint reclaimed from the Greater Victoria Hartland Landfill. Every year Beth and her team distribute free tubs of it, along with kits that include brushes, sponges, information sheets, and the ever-important "Wet Paint" signs. Today, it's fun to wander down the streets here and admire the painted tributes to family members and community leaders, and to see the poetry poles, the family pet poles, and the declarations of love. The poles have become the heartbeat of the community in Fernwood and now around the world.

Address Start at Fernwood & Balmoral Streets, Victoria, BC V8T 2Y1, www.fernwoodnrg.ca | Getting there Bus 22 to Fernwood at Balmoral | Hours Unrestricted | Tip If you'd like to paint a street pole in your own neighbourhood, Island Blue Art and Framing has been around since 1912 and sells paint and fine art paint brushes (905 Fort Street, www.islandblue.monk.ca).

81 Palm Trees in the Breeze

Proof you're in Canada's warmest city

Victorians love phoning their relatives in cities like Saskatoon in January, when the average temperature there is −9°C, to boast about Victoria's weather. The average temperature here in January is a balmy 6.5°C. BC's capital, which is the warmest city in the entire country, is often referred to as "Canada's Banana Belt," and that's why you shouldn't be surprised to see lots of palm trees growing there.

Although these trees are certainly not an indigenous species, the Victoria City Council decided to plant windmill palm trees in the centre of some boulevards leading into town as a way of bragging how warm it is here. The romantic, leafy palms can also be seen in numerous private gardens. Other signs of the mild winters here are smaller and more subtle – and everywhere you look. December often sees certain varieties of rhododendrons blooming, with snowdrops and crocuses popping up in January, and daffodils and tulips debuting in February or March. The rest of Canada is usually still digging out from under heavy snowfalls during those months.

One of the reasons that Victoria's climate is so mild lies in its geography. Located on the southern tip of Vancouver Island, the city is surrounded on three sides by the Pacific Ocean. That ocean maintains a constant temperature of 10°C pretty much year-round. In essence, Victoria is situated next to a giant, aquatic heating blanket during the winter.

The windmill palm variety is pretty much the hardiest palm tree around, which makes it popular in parts of North America – other than Saskatoon. The reason it can tolerate Victoria's winters is because it originates from the cold foothills of the Himalayan Mountains, where it developed a thick fibrous husk. Look for sizable windmill palms on the lawn of a house in Fairfield that has 15 of these trees, the tallest of which is 25 feet high.

Address 428 Kipling Street, Victoria, BC V8S 3J8 | Getting there Bus 7 to Fairfield at Kipling | Hours Unrestricted | Tip Victoria's home gardeners are known to compete for the "ahhhhh" factor with unusual garden displays, like the giant, leafy hedge pruned to look like a choo-choo train (457 Palmer Road).

82 Parliamentary Dining Room
Lunch at the Ledge

Our elected provincial leaders are called Members of the Legislative Assembly (MLAs). They do what most politicians do all day when they get together: they vote on bills, pass laws and debate different issues. They make long speeches, they clap, they boo, they hiss. It's hard physical work as they stand up, sit down, gesture with their hands, pass notes to one another, and check their devices for messages. Doing that kind of intense, calorie-burning work all day, they can build up an appetite. When BC politicians are feeling peckish in parliament, they don't have to wander outside of the beautiful old legislative building to find a nourishing meal. A convenient breakfast or lunch awaits them downstairs in the basement of the Legislature.

There is a little-known and very good, small restaurant that is open to the public in the cellar of the grand old seat of government. The decor is Old World classic, with lots of wood accents and antique furnishings. The food is served on fine china, some of it with the province's logo on it. The servers wear black and white, and the old photos on the walls are also black and white. Getting seated is a bit different than entering your average restaurant though. Your ID is carefully checked, you will need to go through a metal detector, and your bags will be inspected.

Dining here is a memorable experience. In terms of cost, BC politicians don't earn large sums, and so you're likely to pay $22.00 or so for a lunchtime entrée. That's about the same as you would spend at an Earl's, White Spot, or Milestones restaurant. There is absolutely no debate over the quality of the bacon and eggs breakfast. And try the chicken Caesar salad for lunch. Since the daily meal service began, there have been no food fights between the governing political party and members of the official opposition. Well, not yet.

Address 501 Belleville Street, Victoria, BC V8V 1X4, +1 (250) 387-3959, www.leg.bc.ca/content-peo/Pages/Parliamentary-Dining-Room.aspx | Getting there Bus 32, 53 to Legislature Terminal | Hours Mon–Fri 8:30am–3pm, reservation recommended | Tip Across the street from the Legislature is Sequoia Coffee, an amazing coffee shop on the ground floor of the Royal BC Museum in the Pocket Gallery, where museum admission is not required (675 Belleville Street, www.sequoiacoffee.ca).

83 __Peanuts the Horse
A powerful promotional pony

When you first lay eyes on "Peanuts the Horse," two words come to mind: "Giddy Up." This horse is a Victoria icon that's been around over 120 years, which is a long time considering that real horses only live for an average of 25 years. This one is constructed on a wooden frame and covered with burlap and cotton, with a tail and mane made from genuine horsehair. Peanuts is a commercial mannequin resembling a presumably male horse. His storied past tells a tail, or rather tale, of the history of commerce and promotions in Victoria.

Wade Saddlery & Harness store on Johnson Street sold saddles and harnesses, obviously, as well as bridles, reins, and tack. The merchandise had to be displayed in an attractive, compelling manner, and Peanuts was created in 1900 for just this purpose. Though Peanuts had promoted and served the saddle shop well for years, he never had a name. He was eventually sold to the old Kersey Peanut Butter Factory, around 1950. The factory, originally located at 1626 Store Street, then ran a contest to name their new mannequin mascot, which is how Peanuts got his name.

Any horse with this much exposure naturally becomes famous after a century, and Peanuts is no exception. This horse has been featured and photographed for countless magazine and newspaper articles over the years. In 1977 *The Daily Victoria Times Colonist* ran a piece on him, as did *The Islander* in 1983. *Saddle-Up Magazine* even featured him in one of their 2009 editions.

But the horse-trail doesn't end there. From 1977 to 2020, Peanuts was on display at the BC Forestry Discovery Centre in Duncan. In 2020, he was put out to pasture, so to speak, at Heritage Acres, a 29-acre venue run by the Saanich Historical Artefacts Society. Visit the museum here, learn about local life ca. 1900, and then explore the historic buildings and trails. Picnics are encouraged.

Address 7321 Lochside Drive, Saanichton, BC V8M 1W4, +1 (250) 652-5522, www.heritageacresbc.com | Getting there Bus 72 to Island View at Highway 17 | Hours See website for seasonal hours | Tip Harvest Road is an outdoor, farm-to-table restaurant just down the road behind the Michell's Farm Market (2451 Island View Road, Saanichton, www.harvestrd.com).

84_ The Pendray Inn

Time travel for real Victorian living

If H. G. Wells had built his time machine in the living room of the Pendray Inn and travelled to the present day, he would have considered it a failed experiment. Everything here looks exactly as it did when completed in 1897, just two years after *The Time Machine* was published.

The impressive and stately home, now a hotel and restaurant, was built by William Joseph Pendray (1846–1913), who, like many of Victoria's earliest immigrants, arrived here after bouncing around gold mines in California and the Cariboo Mountains. The gold mines made Pendray filthy rich but also filthy dirty. He moved to Victoria, started the colony's first domestic soap company, and became even richer by making other people clean.

Pendray engaged architect Alexander Charles Ewart to build the mansion in the Queen Anne style. A German artist was commissioned to paint frescoes on the ceilings of the parlour, the dining room, and in two of the bedrooms. Panes of stained glass imported from Italy were shipped in barrels of molasses so they wouldn't break, and they were placed throughout the house, a joy for William, his wife Amelia, and their four boys. In 1939, the building left the family's hands. Eventually, the property was purchased and expanded in the 1980s with the construction of the Huntingdon Manor Hotel, styled after the first and finest Canadian Pacific Hotels.

Today, the mansion offers guests the perfect place to relax with an Agatha Christie novel. It is home to one of the most spectacular and authentic tea houses in the country, offering traditional afternoon tea, vegan, and West Coast afternoon teas, and children's tea services. Tarts, profiteroles, scones, macarons, cakes, and jams await your appetite. The number and variety of teas are too many to name but are all TWG Teas from the luxury tea company based in Singapore and served in hand-sewn, cotton tea bags.

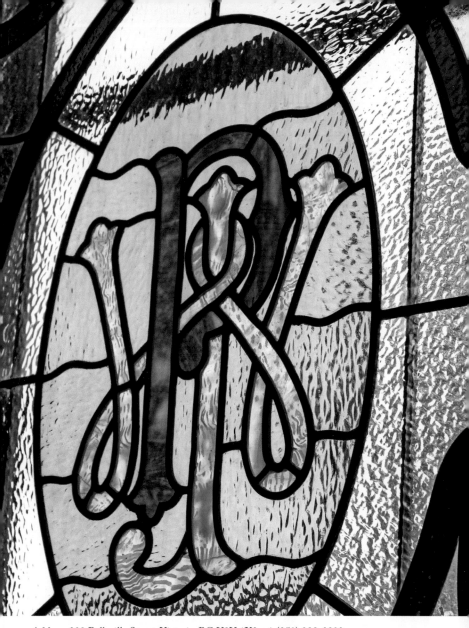

Address 309 Belleville Street, Victoria, BC V8V 1X2, +1 (250) 388-3892,
www.pendrayinnandteahouse.com, info@pendrayinnandteahouse.com | Getting there Bus 2, 5,
to Superior at Montreal | Hours Unrestricted | Tip Across the street is a two-story, white-brick
building, a hidden-in-plain sight artefact of another era that is one of the few remaining
early twentieth-century industrial buildings on Victoria's Inner Harbour. It was built in 1912
and leased to the Canadian Pacific Railway as a linen storage facility for their steamships
(254 Belleville Street).

85 Phillips Tasting Room
The Phoenix Rises

Phillips beer has been around since 2001, and, although it has grown to become a proud brand in British Columbia, it still manages to retain its entrepreneurial character. The brewery was started by a very determined 27-year-old Matt Phillips, who notoriously financed the company on his personal credit cards. Lean days and much nail-biting followed, but the company has now brewed over 300 kinds of beers since it started. You don't have to visit the Phillips tasting room in order to try their beer, but if you like what they've done to please your taste buds, you might want to see what they've done to please your other senses.

The experience begins as you encounter the art deco-styled winged phoenix sign looming over the corner of Government and Discovery Streets, looking something like the chrome hood ornament of a classic American car of the 1950s. In fact, the phoenix logo is a nod to an old brewing company called the Victoria-Phoenix Brewing Company, established in 1893, not far from this location. Then you can enjoy the generous deck outdoors or take in the ambience indoors.

Friendly staff will gladly pour you a fresh one of the sixteen brews on tap or introduce you to their line-up of small-batch distilled spirits; craft brewed, non-alcoholic beer; and house-made sodas and tonics. Snack wise, they have a range of curated bites to pair with your beverage of choice.

They don't take reservations, but the fully accessible and family-friendly venue does occasionally host speakers and events. So consider timing your visit around the scheduled events. Somewhere on the premises, not always on display, is a fully playable beer bottle organ built from an 1886 Chicago pump organ. The "Amazing Philli-phone" beer bottle organ was created by artists Scott Amos and David Parfit, who also fabricated the Musical Railings at Bastion Square Parkade.

Address 2000 Government Street, Victoria, BC V8T 4P1, +1 (250) 380-1912, www.phillipsbeer.com/tasting-room | Getting there Bus 4, 11, 21, 22, 30, 31, 32, 47, 48, 53, 61, 65, 70, 71, 72, 75, 95 to Douglas at Discovery | Hours Sun–Wed noon–8pm, Thu–Sat 11am–9pm | Tip See the original 1888 Victoria Gas Company building just down the street and around the corner (502 Pembroke Street).

86__Playfair Park
Plant decolonisation

You'll want to visit Playfair Park for what it does not have. The dedicated and passionate volunteers tending the grounds of this tiny, two-acre, hilltop gem have worked hard to keep introduced species out. You're in the midst of all native species.

It's worth visiting to go see the camas plants alone – when in bloom, they are the bluest blue you will ever witness. So rich in colour are the native camas plants that in 1849 when he was exploring the Victoria region, Fur Trader James Douglas mistook a field of camas for a lake. The once common and abundant Camas meadows that Douglas saw have, in our modern times, been replaced by development and agriculture.

Another indigenous species that Douglas would have seen in abundance and that has since symbolised Victoria's unique ecosystem is the Garry oak tree. These trees love clinging near or around craggy rock beds, which are abundant in Playfair Park. Garry oaks are as easy to spot as the standout camas, with their distinctly broad and rounded crowns; greyish, brown, scaly bark; and forked stems leading to twisted and gnarled branches. The only place in BC that you'll find this small tree is on the South Coast of Vancouver Island, and intact deep soil Garry oak meadows are very rare today. Restoring them to pre-colonial times has not been an easy task. Colleen O'Brien, one of the main volunteers spearheading the project in collaboration with Saanich Parks, describes it as the first step in a kind of "decolonisation" of the land. She and her dedicated fellow volunteers work hard at getting rid of the invasive species to reveal what is actually there.

The park is a bit out of the way and not that easy to find, and where it's situated feels like a bit of an urban planning afterthought. But once you arrive and discover it, like James Douglas, you will consider it a worthy and fruitful adventure.

Address 1198 Rock Street, Victoria, BC V8P 2B8, www.saanich.ca | Getting there Bus 6, 17 to Quadra at Rock | Hours Daily 8am–11pm | Tip If you feel like a longer walk than the small Playfair Park offers, a few blocks away you'll find a lovely 3.6 km (2.2 mile) wood chip trail that circles Cedar Hill Golf Course. The trail passes through a beautiful old forest and duck ponds – watch for errant golf balls (1040 McKenzie Avenue, www.saanich.ca).

87 __ Point Ellice House
Nothing's changed

Walking into Point Ellice House feels like entering an old, completely furnished family home that's been untouched for almost 50 years. This house has some interesting features. First, the way it came to be is remarkable. In 1975, the O'Reilly family shut the lights off, locked the doors, and left after living there for 108 years. They only took a few personal items with them and left this historic home completely intact, a time capsule in essence. Appliances, clothing, musical instruments, artwork, letters, books, luggage, and dishes – they're all there with over 12,000 personal items.

Many museums today display these types of artifacts from yesteryear, but they are curated and staged. These ones are an authentic domestic family moment frozen in time. John and Inez O'Reilly were approached by a neighbouring industrial complex to give up the land and then ended up selling Point Ellice House to the Province of British Columbia, which turned it into a provincial and national historic site. Built in 1861, it's one of Victoria's oldest homes.

The second interesting aspect is its location. You'd expect such a beautiful home to be in a nice, upscale neighbourhood. Maybe it was a posh residential area back in the 1860s, but today you'll find Point Ellice House smack dab in the middle of a light industrial section of Victoria. You may feel like you are off track or a bit lost when you travel down Hillside Road, past a recycling depot, a compressed gas refuelling station, and a welding shop. Don't stop looking, though, because at the foot of the street, you'll turn left into the driveway of this almost forgotten gem.

Finally, the home's beautiful, almost-two-acre garden is quite special. The family's patriarch Peter O'Reilly was passionate about plants and trees. A must-see is the giant Sequoia that was ordered all the way from San Francisco and planted here in 1876.

Address 2616 Pleasant Street, Victoria, BC V8T 4V3, +1 (250) 380-6506,
www.pointellicehouse.com | Getting there Bus 10 to Bay at Turner | Hours See website
for hours | Tip Not far from Point Ellice House is the Saltchuck Pie Company, an authentic
New Zealand and Australian pie shop that specialises in hot, hand-held, savoury pies
(360 Bay Street, www.saltchuckpies.com).

88 Rudyard Kipling Building
The great author slept here

Rudyard Kipling's poems, short stories, and novels derived their inspiration from many places around the world. One of them was Victoria. He visited the city in 1907 and stayed at the new and then-modern Oak Bay Hotel. Built in 1905, the hotel would have been a mere two years old when he checked in. It was subsequently renamed the Old Charming Inn, and that building was demolished in 1962 to make way for Oak Bay's then most luxurious apartment block, the Rudyard Kipling Building. The front two glass doors today vividly display a capital R and K confirming that one of the great writers from the turn of the last century actually stayed there.

The sweeping ocean view that Kipling enjoyed when he lived there has changed very little. He likely went for long walks in nearby Windsor Park. Or he may have admired the boats across the street on the docks at the Oak Bay Boat House then, replaced by the Oak Bay Marina today.

Kipling (1865–1936), who was also a journalist, wrote *The Jungle Book* in 1894 and went on to win the Nobel Prize in Literature at age 41, making him its youngest recipient to date and the first English-language recipient. He was an adventurer and globetrotter too. Apparently, Kipling fell in love with Victoria, and this is what he wrote about it: "Amongst all the beautiful places in the world, and I think I have seen the most beautiful of them, Victoria ranks the highest."

In his book *Letters of Travel* (1920), he goes on, "To realise Victoria you must take all that the eye admires in Bournemouth, the Isle of Wight and Happy Valley of Hong Kong, the Doon, Sorrento and Camps Bay, and add reminiscences on the Thousand Islands, and arrange the whole around the Bay of Naples, with some Himalayas for the background. Real estate agents recommend it as a little piece of England – the Island on which it stands is about the size of Great Britain."

Address 1420 Beach Drive, Victoria, BC V8S 2N8 | Getting there Bus 2, 8 to Newport at Windsor | Hours Unrestricted from the outside | Tip If you are a true fan of Kipling, then take a brief, four-block stroll along Kipling Street in the Fairfield neighbourhood (Kipling Street between Richardson Street & Fairfield Road).

89__The Rockhound Shop
Dig this

A rockhound is someone who specialises in geology or is an amateur rock or mineral collector. How can you identify true rockhounds? Here's one way: After picking up rocks, they often lick them to bring out all the natural colours.

The best places to find interesting rocks in Victoria are rock quarries, road cuts, riverbanks, creek beds, and beaches. Gardens with fresh overturned soil, and Victoria has many, are also good places to start looking and licking. But you can save yourself a lot of time by going to "the source" in downtown Victoria: The Rockhound Shop.

Rockhound has been in the same location on Cloverdale Avenue since 1967. And it's a perfect place and building for a rock shop: a simple, white-brick structure with a green roof, sitting on top of a small grassy hill, with a big parking lot, and lots and lots of rocks in the window. They sell rocks, minerals, fossils, crystals, and rockhounding and metal detection equipment. If you find a rock that you can't identify, just bring it in, and the staff here will do their best to help you figure out what it is.

Just browsing through the shelves in the eclectic shop is a bit like prospecting. Like many Chinese settlers did in British Columbia in 1866, you'll discover some jade. British Columbia is world famous for it, and the shop has plenty on hand. It is a little-known fact that a lot of the world's jade comes from this province. The Government even proclaimed jade as its Official Provincial Stone in 1969. The petrified wood is worth seeking out too. It is created over hundreds of thousands of years when minerals, including silica from volcanic ash, is absorbed into porous wood. The rockstar display of the shop, though, has to be the amethyst geodes. Some people believe these large, purple crystals will absorb negative energy and create an air of tranquillity in their surrounding environment.

Address 777 Cloverdale Avenue, Victoria, BC V8X 2S6, +1 (250) 475-2080, www.rockhoundshop.com, rockhoundshop@gmail.com | Getting there Bus 30, 31, 32, 47, 48 to Douglas at Cloverdale | Hours Tue–Sat 10am–5pm | Tip Studio 37, kitty corner to the Rockhound shop, is a small art studio that features the sculptures of Armando Barbon and other artists in residence with whom Barbon collaborates (800 Cloverdale Avenue, www.studio37.ca).

90 Ross Bay Cemetery

Very Victorian graves of great Victorians

The Victorian era is known for its eclectic design style in all manner of things, and you'll find many examples of that style among the tomb-stones at the Ross Bay Cemetery. In addition to the great funereal archi-tecture, you'll see the final resting place of many notable names in Canadian history. For example, John Hamilton Gray (1814–1889), the only "father of Confederation" buried in Western Canada, is here. The Colony of British Columbia's first Black police constable Lorne Lewis (1814–1912) rests here. Chief James Squameyuqs (1797–1892), second Chief of the Songhees, is buried here under the name James Siomax. Look around, and you'll also find graves of some of the people men-tioned in other chapters of this book, including Dr. James Helmcken, Robert Dunsmuir, Emily Carr, and David Fee.

One of the most creative markers that you certainly ought not to miss on your amble through this pastoral park is the bronze fireman's helmet resting on a cement pillow – the final resting place for Fred Medley (1892–1925), whom the local newspaper described as a "faithful and highly regarded employee of the Victoria fire depart-ment ... very popular with the firemen." One look at his grave marker, and you know that was true.

There are plenty more interesting tombstones to see: the Wilson Family marker includes a bird because Victoria Jane Wilson left her fortune to her brandy-loving parrot. George W. Battersby (1855–1910) has a tombstone shaped like a heart. A. J. Hay (1858–1901) has a tombstone shaped like a tree-stump.

Finally, make sure you visit the grave of Isabella Mainville Ross (1808–1885). Wife of Hudson's Bay trader Charlie Ross, she was also the original owner of the cemetery and the first registered in-dependent woman landowner in British Columbia. But the oldest grave here belongs to Mary Letitia (Pemberton) Pearse (1840–1872).

Address 1495 Fairfield Road, Victoria, BC V8S 5L8, +1 (250) 598-8870, www.oldcem.bc.ca/cem/cem_rb | **Getting there** Bus 3, 7 to Fairfield at Stannard; Fred Medley's fire helmet grave marker is located near the middle of the cemetery | **Hours** Unrestricted | **Tip** Nearby Ross Bay Villa, built in 1865, is the home of the Old Cemeteries Society, which has an interesting museum (1490 Fairfield Road, www.rossbayvilla.org).

91 The Roxy
Historic Quadra Quonset hut

You don't see a lot of Quonset huts these days, and when you do, it's usually the modern kind used for storing farm equipment. But here on Quadra Street, you can see one of the old-school, vintage kind of huts. This structure dates at least back to 1949, when George Walkey and Ed Nixon used it to open The Fox movie theatre. The domed movie den provided local film fans with 30 x 12 metres (100 x 40 feet) of movie-viewing spaciousness, complete with a new projector and modern seats for 450 people. Tickets for the cheap seats were 15 cents. Walkey ran the pharmacy across the street. Nixon was the projectionist.

The origins of this specific Quonset hut are murky, but the structure owes its heritage to war. The Quonset hut is based on the design of the Nissen Hut, which is named after its inventor Lt. Colonel Peter Nissen, a Canadian officer in the Royal Engineers during World War I. The Quonset hut is basically the same thing but named after Quonset Point at the Davisville Naval Construction Battalion Center in Davisville, Rhode Island. That's where the US Navy started making them during World War II. The key feature of these huts is that they were cheaply made and easily transported. Legend holds the Nissen hut could be packed in a standard army wagon and erected by six men in four hours.

This hut has had its ups and downs and a variety of owners since Walkey and Nixon sold it in 1966 to a guy who dipped into the adult movie genre when times got tough. To distance itself from that cultural low, the name was changed to Quadra Theatre in the 1970s. In the next decade a trio of business partners bought the hut and changed the name to The Roxy Cinegog, a play on the word synagogue, for devout worshipers of the silver screen. It became the Roxy Classic Theatre in 2007 and continued to show movies until 2013. That's when it became what it is today: home to the Blue Bridge Theatre Company.

Address 2657 Quadra Street, Victoria, BC V8T 4E3, +1 (250) 382-3370, www.attheroxy.ca | Getting there Bus 4, 6, 9 to Hillside at Quadra | Hours Unrestricted from the outside; see website for events schedule | Tip Directly across the street, visit the hip Quadra neighbourhood restaurant and bar Part and Parcel for "handcrafted cooking" (2656 Quadra Street, www.partandparcel.ca).

92 Saanich Historical Society
Tractor attraction

While driving by the Saanich Historical Society sign, almost everyone from Victoria curiously peers out of their car window – and keeps on going. Tourists arriving by ferry and then driving down the Pat Bay Highway also pass the rusty old tractors and combines in the huge farm field. If they notice the antique *Heritage Acres* sign, they may jot it down on their long list of things to do in the Capitol. Three words of advice to locals and tourists alike: Stop and Go! It's amazing.

What you don't see from the highway are the 29-acres of forest and farmland, and the thousands of artefacts. Since 1967, the society has been restoring and preserving farm equipment from a bygone era. Over the years, they have amassed Western Canada's largest collection of harvesting gear, steam equipment, water pumps, and blacksmith equipment. There is even an entire authentic and operational old saw-mill on site. Once you have spent a bit of time wandering around the grounds, you'll understand why all that space is required to truly convey what rural life was like on the Saanich Peninsula 100 years ago.

But it's the old tractors that are the central core of the operation. They come in all different shapes, colours, and sizes. They have different patinas and weathered signs of wear and tear. They emit a variety of smells as they are fired up, and they make different sounds. To appreciate and understand tractors, you need to see them operating outdoors in a field.

To truly value tractors, you need to see men and women tinkering with their engines, adjusting and fine tuning them, and fixing them. That's what the volunteers at Heritage Acres do all the time, but don't expect lots of interpretative signage here. The place is a bit scattered and a tad disorganised, but that just adds to its charm and mysticism. It's so much better than being inside a museum, and definitely worth the stop.

Address 7321 Lochside Drive, Saanichton, BC V8M 1W4, +1 (250) 652 5522, www.heritageacresbc.com, info@heritageacresbc.com | **Getting there** By car, take Highway 17, turn west onto Island View Road, then north on Lochside Drive | **Hours** See website for seasonal hours | **Tip** You'll find hundreds of free-flying butterflies at the nearby Victoria Butterfly Gardens, along with parrots, frogs, and lots of lush indoor jungle plants (1461 Benvenuto Avenue, Brentwood Bay, www.butterflygardens.com).

93 Sailboat Racing Off Cattle Point

Royal racing

Racing sailboats is a test of skill, courage, and endurance. There's nothing like competitive sailing with a breezy westerly at your back and surrounded by choppy waves, while feeling the salty wind in your hair as you hoist the spinnaker. But if you can't race sailboats, the next best thing is to watch them race. And the closer the better.

Every Wednesday evening during the summer near Cattle Point, the Royal Victoria Yacht Club stages sailboat races. The strong currents in the waters adjacent to Cattle Point swirl in large circles. Think of the concept of water churning clockwise around your sink after you pull the plug, and that will give you an idea of the strength of these challenging waters. This means that the sailboats end up repeatedly speeding by, jostling for position, often looking for tide relief very close to the shoreline. It's really exciting to watch the drama and thrill of competitive sailing unfold right in front of you. Most of the races begin at 6:15pm, and you will have no problem hearing the starter's pistol fire as the dozens of aggressive windjammers try to outmanoeuvre one another for an early lead.

Competitive sailors, a small nascent local yacht club, and Queen Victoria all got into the same boat together, figuratively speaking, way back in 1888. That's when 11 eager yachtsmen decided to celebrate the queen's birthday with a commemorative sailboat race. That race became the catalyst for the formation of the Victoria Yacht Club in 1892, when 46 sailing enthusiasts banded together to extend the sailing season beyond the queen's birthday. But this prestigious and historic club's royal roots go even deeper. In 1911, as the club continued to grow in size and stature, King George V granted permission for them to add the prefix "Royal" to their title. Make sure to give the sailboats the royal wrist wave as they go quickly sailing by.

Address Cattle Point, 1 Scenic Drive, Victoria, BC, www.rvyc.bc.ca/Racing | Getting there
Bus 5 to Estevan at Beach, then walk 10 minutes to Cattle Point | Hours Unrestricted | Tip
The visually striking Oak Bay Cenotaph, perhaps Victoria's most unique, rests under a tall
flagpole on a hill directly behind the Cattle Point parking lot. Erected in 1948, it features
Mother Peace looking down, her loving arms protecting the 97 names of Oak Bay's 1939–1945
war dead (2800 Beach Drive, www.oakbay.ca/explore-oak-bay).

94   Sidewalk of Sorrow
Where Wheelan shot Fee instead of Deasy

Most Canadians know that Member of Parliament Thomas D'Arcy McGee was assassinated in Ottawa by an Irish Republican in 1868. Few know that a similar assassination kind of happened here in 1890, on this sidewalk outside St. Andrews' Cathedral.

The triggerman at the centre of this story is construction worker Laurence Whelan. He had attended a workers' celebration here two months earlier, when the cornerstone for the church was laid. Flags had been brought out for the festive occasion: the British flag, out of respect for the crown; the American flag, out of respect for the many American workers engaged in the project; and the Irish flag, out of respect for the many Irish Canadians and Irish Americans who had been working on the site. But when someone put up a flag promoting Irish independence, the foreman, Thomas Deasy, wary of the violence that had shaken Ottawa years earlier, had it taken down. Whelan didn't like this very much and vowed to make Deasy pay.

Knowing Deasy was a churchgoer, and knowing he usually wore a white overcoat, Whelan planned to intercept him when he left church on Christmas Eve. Sure enough, lurking Whelan eventually saw a man in a white overcoat leave the church. He approached, raised his shotgun, and fired point blank. The man dropped to the ground, his overcoat smoking. Except the man wasn't Deasy. It was shopkeeper David Fee.

At his trial, Whelan argued he had not attempted to kill Deasy over politics but had only meant to frighten Fee with a blank round because he had seen Fee being disrespectful and rowdy outside the church. The judge didn't buy the bizarre defence, but the jury did. Whelan was convicted of manslaughter, not murder.

David Fee's funeral was the most attended in Victoria's short history. He is buried at Ross Bay Cemetery, where some say his ghost appears in a white raincoat, still seeking justice.

Address St. Andrew's Cathedral, 740 View Street, Victoria, BC VW8 1J8, +1 (250) 388-5571, www.standrewscathedral.com | **Getting there** Bus 4, 6, 7, 11, 22 to Douglas at View | **Hours** Unrestricted | **Tip** The top of the unique altar in St. Andrew's Cathedral was built by acclaimed artist and master carver Charles Elliot of the T'sartlip First Nation. It's made from yellow cedars weighing about 400 pounds and rests on two traditional indigenous "bentwood boxes."

95 The Signs of Lekwungen
Whorls of culture

The Signs of Lekwungen (pronounced Le-KWUNG-en) are a series of seven art installations that designate culturally significant sites of the Songhees and Esquimalt Nations along the Inner Harbour and other locations in Victoria. The markers, created in 2008, are bronze castings of original cedar carvings that were conceptualised and carved by Coast Salish artist and master carver Butch Dick with his sons Clarence and Bradley helping on two of them. Each of the markers is about 2.5 metres (8 feet) high and weighs a little over 450 kg (992 pounds). If they look like spindle whorls to you, then you guessed right. The markers actually do represent the spindle whorls that were traditionally used by Coast Salish women to spin wool. They were considered to be the foundation of a Coast Salish family.

This marker at Songhees Point is called *PAH-lu-tsuss* (which means "cradleboard"). "Traditionally, once infants had learned to walk, their cradles were placed at this sacred headland because of the spiritual power of the water," according to the Songhees Nation's website. More recently, there was a settlement here, and subsequently a Songhees reserve, which traded with the fort on the opposite shore. The Songhees Nation moved from this reserve to their current reserve in 1911. Underneath the marker, there's a sandblasted map of the Inner Harbour, illustrating the locations of the six other markers.

As you tour around Victoria, look for the other markers, as they're all quite distinct. The one at the north side of the Malahat Building on Wharf Street recognizes colonisation; the one outside City Hall represents a respected speaker; another at the lower causeway of Inner Harbour has an eagle theme; sea otters are featured on the one at Beacon Hill; the one outside the Royal BC Museum celebrates diversity; and another at Laurel Point has a Four Winds theme. All the original carvings are in the foyer of City Hall.

Address 50 Songhees Road, Victoria, BC V9A 7J4, +1 (250) 361-0246, www.victoria.ca, culture@victoria.ca | Getting there Bus 10, 15, 25 to Esquimalt at Tyee | Hours Unrestricted | Tip Nearby is the *Spirit of Lekwammen* totem pole, raised here in 1994 for the 15th Commonwealth Games, which were officially opened in Victoria by Queen Elizabeth II.

96 Sitting Lady Falls

Victoria's most beautiful waterfall

Hikes with a purpose are the best kind. Routes that are close to town, short, and on well-groomed trails give you every excuse to go walking, especially if you want to see one of the most beautiful waterfalls in Victoria with a great name and unusual waterflow.

With so much water rushing down steep hills, rocky moss outcroppings, and small mountains around Victoria, the region can boast being home to half a dozen great waterfalls. Sitting Lady Falls in Witty's Lagoon Regional Park looks like a sitting lady, kind of. You and your friends can take the 500-metre (.3-mile) walk from the parking lot to the wooden viewing platform and decide for yourselves. Comments like, "I can almost see it," and "If I squint my eyes – well maybe," or "No way" will fill the crisp seaside air as you decide for yourselves.

Ice-cold water flows down a steep crevasse in one cascading stream, hits the rocks below, and divides into two rapidly descending, swirling, white chutes. The two identical chutes look like a lady's legs, and where the water lands above them could be her hips in a seated position. The flowing water stream above that could be her upper trousseau, poetically speaking. Like most waterfalls on Vancouver Island, this one is best visited in the winter. Late fall and early spring are good too, but if you go in the summer months, it is too dried up to get the sitting lady effect.

After viewing the falls, spend some time walking around Witty's Lagoon. Over 160 species of birds live in this vibrant rain forest, and it has the most amazing beaches. Large salt marshes, offshore islets, an interesting sand dune ecosystem, and gnarly driftwood everywhere are just a few of the other highlights. So, if you've never hiked to see a waterfall, Sitting Lady, which is so easy to get to and in such a beautiful setting, should be your first – but not your last.

Address 3920 Metchosin Road, Metchosin, BC V9C 4A5, www.crd.bc.ca/parks-recreation-culture/parks-trails | Getting there Bus 54 to Metchosin at Duke Road W | Hours Unrestricted | Tip The Falls are in a rural area with no shops except for Crazy Cookie House, right next door to the Sitting Lady Falls parking lot, housed in a crooked, little, storybook building that kids love (4105 Metchosin Road, Metchosin, www.morello.ca/crazycookie).

97 The Six Mile Pub

Postal pub crawl

The Six Mile Pub, which was founded in 1855, is actually British Columbia's oldest pub. It has a lively vibe and boasts a couple of fireplaces, a pool table room, lots of comfy seating, and tons of historical artefacts and black-and-white photos. In the summertime its huge outdoor patio overlooking a creek on a leafy gorge is the perfect spot.

There are two other pubs in town that have very similar names. Visitors and locals who spot the three old pubs around Victoria may assume that they are all part of a chain. After all, their names sound the same: the Four-Mile House, the Six-Mile Pub, and the Seventeen-Mile House Pub. They all have similar rustic Tudor designs. But they are independent businesses that are not connected. Then why the similar names?

140 years ago, these pubs were known as "roadhouses," and they were the hubs of their respective communities, providing postal addresses for those who lived close by. In the 1880s, when stagecoaches began mail service, these pubs marked the distances from the Central Victoria Post Office to each outpost, hence the numbers in these three pubs' names.

Mail delivery was only one essential service they offered. They also provided a place for weary travellers to rest. They were sometimes used as temporary schools, or as places for civic meetings and church services. One of them is even reported to have served as a brothel. As the years progressed into the 1920s and phone service was introduced, the roadhouses eventually became another communications hub offering this ultra-modern convenience too.

Today, a large clientele of locals, people from the city core, and travellers from all around the world still come to the Six-Mile and the other two pubs to share a meal and a drink. Just don't expect them to receive and hang onto your mail for you. And their pay phone, it vanished years ago, just like the stagecoaches.

Address 494 Island Highway, Victoria, BC V9B 1H5, www.sixmilepub.com | Getting there Bus 39, 46, 48, 51, 53, 61, 95 to Island Highway at Six Mile Road | Hours Mon–Thu 11am–9pm, Fri & Sat 11am–10 pm, Sun 11am–8pm | Tip Take a leisurely waterfront stroll through nearby Parsons Bridge Park, which features a beautiful untouched natural state trail along the Parsons Cove Inlet (www.viewroyal.ca/EN/main/discover/parks-recreation/parks.html).

98__ The Temple Building
The oldest continuously used commercial building

Many other cities established around the same time as Victoria have had their oldest buildings go up in smoke (Vancouver), fall to the ground (San Francisco), or be on the wrong side of the wrecking ball (Seattle). Of those that have survived, many have had several lives, morphing from commercial to residential use, to storage facility, to some other function. The Temple Building stands apart from all these others as it remains standing, and it is and has always been used as office space. And not only that, it is widely acclaimed as an architectural jewel and certainly one of Victoria's most architecturally significant buildings.

The key features to look for are the distinctive brick walls rising from the sandstone base and its rounded entry arch with impressive relief terracotta ornamentation. Above that main arch, look for the name plaque inscribed, *Temple Building*. Motifs of stylized and natural foliage adorn the building at the cornice level, above the entry arch, along the string courses (a decorative band on the exterior of a building), above windows, and in several attractive medallion insets.

Incredibly, Samuel Maclure, the architect who designed this building, was just 33 years old when it was completed in 1893. His patron was an older and more established man, Robert Ward. Ward was an enterprising businessman who started out in the import and export business and then branched out into insurance. He commissioned the Temple Building for his business, Robert Ward & Company. However, his determination to have it built despite an economic recession, a smallpox epidemic, and a real estate crisis soon made it a shining example of Ward's faith in a brighter and more prosperous future for the city. When you admire this building, marvel at its design, its longevity, and the inspiration it gave to a young city still uncertain of its future.

Address 535 Fort Street, Victoria, BC V8W 1H9 | **Getting there** Bus 14, 15 to Fort at Wharf | **Hours** Unrestricted from the outside only | **Tip** If you think this is impressive, visit Rappahannock, another one of Samuel Maclure's eye-popping architectural designs. It's a Tudor Revival British Arts and Crafts home built for prominent realtor Herbert Bowen in 1910 (1595 Rockland Avenue).

99 The Terry Fox Monument
Remembering a true Canadian hero

It's a statue that commemorates Canada's greatest hero. It marks the exact spot of a dream that was never realised at the time, but nevertheless a dream that lived on to become something bigger than Terry Fox could ever have imagined.

Terry Fox (July 28, 1958–June 28, 1981) was a Canadian athlete, a world-renowned humanitarian, and a cancer research activist – a true Canadian, whose reputation has gone on to transcend generations. It wouldn't be a stretch to say that Fox represents the heart and soul of Canada. In 1980 after his right leg was amputated due to cancer, he began his ambitious cross-Canada Marathon of Hope with the goal of running 7,250 kilometres (4,500 miles) from coast to coast. Beginning near St. John's in Newfoundland, he dipped his right leg into the icy Atlantic Ocean and filled up two bottles with seawater. He planned to keep one as a souvenir and pour the other one into the Pacific Ocean when the tour was complete, near the site where his statue stands today.

Sadly, that dream would not come true. After 143 days of running the equivalent of a 26-mile marathon every day, the horrible cancer returned, this time to his lungs. Fox had to stop running in Thunder Bay, Ontario. His financial goal to raise 24 million dollars, one dollar for each Canadian at the time, has since been far surpassed. To date, over 850 million dollars have been raised in his name. Every year millions of people from 25 countries around the world participate in annual Terry Fox Runs and fund-raising events.

The tour was about more than just raising money though. Through his heroic efforts, Terry Fox has inspired generations of Canadians. Fourteen schools across Canada bear his name, and over 32 roads and streets are also named after him. The statue erected in 2005 at the south-west corner of Beacon Hill Park is the work of the artist Nathan Scott.

"Somewhere the hurting must stop..."

TERRY FOX
1958 – 1981

Address Dallas Road & Douglas Street, Victoria, BC V8V 0B9, www.readtheplaque.com/plaque/terry-fox-mile-0 | Getting there Bus 2, 3, 5 to Niagara at Douglas | Hours Unrestricted | Tip Three blocks up the street, you'll find a Victoria food lovers' institution, The Beacon Drive Restaurant, serving up burgers, shakes, sandwiches, onion rings, soft serve ice cream, and more since 1958. For 28 years in a row, they have been voted the best place to go in Victoria for ice cream (126 Douglas Street, www.beacondrivein.ca/Home).

100   The *Tilikum* Voyage Plaque

The Nootkan canoe that went around the world

Imagine sailing around the world in a canoe. Crazy, right? Not in the mind of a 43-year-old ship's carpenter named John Voss. In 1901, Voss decided that he would make that voyage himself. He purchased a 38-foot (12-metre) Nootkan (Nuu-chah-nulth) canoe for the task. The vessel, a dugout canoe made from a large red cedar log about a hundred years previously, was then fitted with three sailing masts, christened *Tilikum*, meaning "Friends" in Chinook Wawa language, and made ready to sail across the Pacific.

Voss found an ideal canoe mate in 25-year-old Oak Bay journalist Norman K. Luxton. From Manitoba, Luxton had very little experience on the high seas, but he had true grit and a thirst for aventure. You can find the plaque commemorating the day Voss and Luxton set sail for England on May 20, 1901.

It's a long colourful story, but the short version is that Voss achieved his goal, reaching Margate by 1904. Luxton only made it as far as Fiji. He fell overboard, got cut up by corral, and had to call it quits. Voss then went through a series of mates, including the "Tattooed Man of Australia," a former member of Robert Scott's South Polar Expedition. At every stop, Voss exhibited the canoe and soon became a media sensation. People were astounded by the idea that anyone could possibly navigate such a craft such a distance. It was a feat of derring-do that thrilled and stimulated the imaginations of Europeans and branded the West Coast as a land of mystery and adventure.

It's remarkable that the *Tilikum* survives to this day. After sitting unwanted and derelict in the Thames River for nearly 30 years, she was finally repatriated to Victoria by the BC Government. In 1965, the Maritime Museum of BC took her into its care.

Address 1270 Beach Drive, Victoria, BC V8S 2N3 | Getting there Bus 1, 2 to Newport at Orchard | Hours Unrestricted | Tip Oak Bay Marina is a stone's throw away and a great place to start your own watery adventures. Ask about renting a paddleboard or a kayak, or booking a kayak tour (1327 Beach Drive, www.oakbaymarina.com).

101 Trans-Canada Highway Mile Zero

Get your kicks on Route One

The Trans-Canada Highway is the backbone of this great nation. The mainly four lane, two-way motorway, which was completed in 1962, is exactly 7,821 kilometres (4,860 miles) from Coast to Coast. Mile Zero is marked by a lovely stone and wooden monument in Beacon Hill Park. That would lead one to believe that on the other side of the country, four and a half time zones away, there's a corresponding marker depicting mile 4,860. But no, in downtown St. John's Newfoundland you'll find another prominent marker also claiming to be "Mile Zero." You are probably wondering now, where is the halfway point on the highway. That's easy and undisputable: it is 40 miles west of Sault Ste. Marie, Ontario. It had a sign marking it that was stolen for reasons that remain a mystery. But it eventually resurfaced on Kijiji, being sold by a man in Edmonton who picked it up at a garage sale.

For decades the fortified marker in Victoria has been the site of countless pictures of people posing before they embark on cross-Canada driving, walking, or cycling trips. When you visit the marker, which is a stone's throw from the Pacific Ocean, don't be surprised if a group of cyclists approaches you to take a picture of them standing in front of the sign, right after they have followed tradition and dipped their wheels in the sea. Every year about 5,000 to 6,000 people pedal across Canada on a trip that takes about 111 days. The trips are mainly done in the summer, when the prevailing winds blow west to east, adding validity to the premise that the Victoria marker has a tad more authenticity.

The Trans-Canada Highway, also referred to as Highway One, is Canada's version of Route 66 in the US. Both iconic roads wend their ways through many small towns and lead curious travelers to find bizarre civic markers and monuments.

Address Dallas Road & Douglas Street, Victoria, BC V8V 0B9, www.tourismvictoria.com | **Getting there** Bus 2, 3, 5 to Niagara at Douglas | **Hours** Unrestricted | **Tip** A short walk south of the Mile Zero Marker is a wooden and metal anchor on a hill near the shore that the City of Victoria recently installed as an attraction. They admit to knowing nothing about its history and have put out a plea on Twitter (www.twitter.com/cityofvictoria) for information on its origin. Go have a look and see if you know where it came from.

102__Trestles of Lockwood Trail

A trail and two trestles

Canada's early cities were once laced with railway tracks. At the time, the railways were the model of progress: efficient, affordable, and, in the case of the electric railways, very "green." From the late 1800s to the mid-1950s, they were everywhere. But then they went out of style and became abandoned, leaving strange gaps between buildings downtown and overgrown paths across the countryside. The good news is that many of these tracks are now coming back into service in the form of bike paths and walking or running trails.

The 29-kilometre (18-mile) Lochside Trail runs along the route of what was once the Canadian Pacific Northern Railway (CPNR) system, built in 1917. The original CPNR service ran from downtown Victoria up past North Quadra, through Cordova Bay, and out to Patricia Bay at a terminal near Lockside Drive. At the Victoria end to the South, the trail connects to the Galloping Goose Trail. Bikers looking for a pleasant, generally flat route with a mix of scenery will enjoy the Lochside Trail and its two unique features: the wooden trestles at Blenkinsop Lake and at Swan Lake.

The Swan Lake trestle was restored at the end of the last century and runs next to a lake and wetlands teeming with natural wonders. The 181 bird species in the area include loons, cranes, plovers, ducks, geese, and, yes, swans. At the Blenkinsop Lake Trestle, about 2 kilometres (1.25 miles) north, look for the life-size sculpture *Old Farmer Roy Hawes* by Victoria artist Nathan Scott. The District of Saanich commissioned this piece in 2001. Roy Hawes was a retired local farmer, and the statue of him serves as a tribute to all the early farmers who made their livelihood in the Blenkinsop area. Scott also created the Terry Fox sculpture at mile 0 of the Trans-Canada Highway.

Address Lochside Regional Trail, Victoria, BC V8X 4A5, www.gallopinggoosetrail.com/pdf/lochside_trail_guide.pdf | **Getting there** Bus 26 to Saanich at Lodge | **Hours** Unrestricted | **Tip** The Swan Lake Nature House is an interpretive information centre that gives a fresh and engaging take on the natural wonders in and around Swan Lake (3873 Swan Lake Road, www.swanlake.bc.ca).

103__ The Union Club

Where the elite meet

Back in the days before Facebook, LinkedIn, and the like, if a fellow wanted to present his hot takes on the affairs of the day, complain about the government, sniff out investors for a new enterprise, plot some scheme to hike to the North pole, or simply wanted to get away from whatever it was he wanted to avoid, he would go to his club and hang out with his social network. Well, he would if he was a gentleman in the late 1800s.

In London, England, there were clubs like Boodle's, The East India Club, The Reform Club, The Athenaeum, and White's. All sorts of movers and shakers belonged to these clubs. In Victoria, they belonged to The Union Club. Members have included the political, economic, and social power of the province since the club was founded in 1879. But not all were great Canadians. In 1870, when the Colony of BC was debating whether it should join the Confederation, the club's second president, Montague William Tyrwhitt-Drake, was against the idea. Rising in the Legislature Building, he said, "I do not trust the politicians of Ottawa. I do not desire to give them the power to raise money upon our vast and rich territory, whilst we should get nothing from Canada in return. I would rather remain as we are …."

Other members from yesteryear remain well-known to this day. In the 1920s, the club's president was businessman Robert Pim Butchart, whose wife Jennie famously converted his rock quarry into the stunning Butchart Gardens. The club's first woman president, Grace Van Den Brink, was installed in 2019.

The building's solid yet detailed Italian Renaissance Revival style; its numerous, fine terra cotta design elements; its regal entrance portico on the west side; and its unique, curved bay on the side all combine to project an impressive image of historic power and wealth.

Address 805 Gordon Street, Victoria, BC V8W 1Z6, +1 (250) 384-1151, www.unionclub.com, info@unionclub.com | **Getting there** Bus 2, 3, 5, 10, 30, 31, 32, 47, 48, 53, 61, 65, 70, 71, 72, 75, 95 to Douglas at Courtney | **Hours** Unrestricted from the outside only | **Tip** Across the street is the Belmont Building, also built in 1912 and one of the first buildings in Victoria to use concrete in its construction. Robert Buchart once had office space here when he was president of the British Columbia Cement Company (801 Government Street).

104 The Victoria Bug Zoo

North America's largest tropical insect collection

The best thing about the Victoria Bug Zoo is not the bugs, although they are great, but the people who work there. They love bugs. They love talking about bugs, and they love showing you bugs in their glass cages. They even love handing you bugs. That's right. They will place living green, brown, and black bugs in your hands. This Zoo is hands-on in every sense of the word. There's always a friendly enthusiastic educator standing nearby to explain these amazing creatures' habits and habitats.

With over 50 different species on hand, so to speak, give yourself at least an hour to explore this small and unique home to insects, arachnids, and anthropoids. You will see tarantulas, cockroaches, scorpions, walking sticks, millipedes, and even some very cool praying mantis, to name just a few. They also host Canada's largest ant farm, displaying the lives of leaf cutter ants.

If you didn't get a chance to see the Beatles during their seven appearances in Canada in the 1960s, don't worry. You can see some Asian beetles here. Unlike the Fab Four, these scary looking, white-eyed, beetles sit on small logs in their aquariums, seemingly poised to attack at any moment. It is fun to watch them push each other out of the way as they crawl around their environment. With their contrasting white markings, they are really easy to spot.

The same thing cannot be said for the Stick Bugs. With their slender camouflaged legs, their muddy, greenish-brown bodies, and their ability to stay almost perfectly still, you will have to look hard to distinguish them from the plants they are perched on. The spiders at the Bug Zoo come in all sizes, with the large ones almost unable to fit into the palm of your hand.

Afraid of bugs? Don't worry. One of the aims of the Bug Zoo is to help people get over their fears of insects in a relaxed, non-threatening, and safe environment.

Address 631 Courtney Street, Victoria, BC V8W 1B8, +1 (250) 384-2847, www.victoriabugzoo.ca, bugs@victoriabugzoo.ca | **Getting there** Bus 2, 3, 5, 10, 30, 31, 32, 47, 48, 53, 61, 65, 70, 71, 72, 75, 95 to Douglas at Courtney | **Hours** Mon–Fri 11am–4pm, Sat&Sun 10am–4pm | **Tip** Spend time with a large mural depicting Queen Victoria just around the corner from the Bug Zoo. It goes to great length exploring the question, "Did Queen Victoria even know that in 1843 The Hudson's Bay Company decided to name this fur trading post after her?" (914 Gordon Street).

105___ Wheelies

Where gearheads gather

Is it a café, a diner, a roadhouse, or a garage? The answer is yes. It is all those things. If you want to buy a chopper and also chomp on a chicken sandwich, Wheelies Motorcycles is the place where you can do both.

It's set well back from the street, behind a chain-link fence and a parking lot, so you might drive right past it. But the big, black lettering across the front of the white two-story building that says *WHEELIES MOTORCYCLES* should clue you in that you're in the right place. Don't be intimidated by the choppers resting outside. Pretend you're a character played by Peter Fonda, Patrick Swayze, Tom Cruise, or Marlon Brando, and walk right in. Put to rest any thoughts you might be accosted for trespassing by a bearded dude with a spanner – the staff are very friendly, the grub is good, and there are plenty of non-bikers, who are also here to enjoy the scene.

Park yourself on the extensive patio and congratulate yourself for finding the part of Victoria you never read about in the tourist guides. You'll find no tea or scones here.

Instead, the menu offers hearty sandwiches and no-fuss comfort food, like mac-n-cheese. Ask for some Hot Wheelies hot sauce. On the walls, you'll see miscellaneous chrome and classic motor-cycle photos. On the shelves and in display cabinets, you'll find a wide variety of interesting items to help you express your biker style: baseball shirts, t-shirts, snapback hats, beanies, jackets, jeans, and everything in between.

Wheelies comes by its style honestly. The building used to be an auto repair shop in the late 1940s, and the garage door you walk through is not a retrofit – it's the real deal. To the left, right, and all around it are industrial buildings and businesses that speak to the unpretentious and authentic nature of the Rock Bay neighbourhood. Immerse yourself in the biker vibe and roll on in.

Address 2620 Rock Bay Avenue, Victoria, BC V8T 4R9, +1 (250) 995-9359, www.wheeliesmotorcycles.ca, wheelies@wheeliesmotorcycles.ca | Getting there Bus 10 to Bay at Rock Bay | Hours Tue–Thu, Sat & Sun 11am–5pm, Fri 11am–9pm | Tip Go see the nearby Rock Bay Mural Project, a collaborative effort between First Nations communities, government, and industry (Government and Pembroke Streets, www.rockbaymural.com).

106 The William Head Federal Penitentiary

Club Fed

Jails are generally built inland in isolated, far-off, rural settings. It makes sense for security reasons. It also makes sense from an economical point of view to locate prisons where land is cheaper. Of all the federal penitentiaries in Canada, one really stands out for its unusual location. This minimum-security federal institution for men is 25 kilometres (15.5 miles) southwest of Victoria on the southernmost tip of Vancouver Island. About 100 prisoners live there today, half serving life sentences. But what makes this prison so unique is its stunning waterfront location.

Breathtaking ocean vistas, the sound of crashing waves against the shoreline, sandy beaches, whale watching, plus a host of other sights make the residential properties close to the William Head Institution very desirable places to visit, or, even better, to live. The locals call it "Club Fed." That moniker refers to the worldwide chain of all-inclusive luxury resorts around the world called Club Med. Not far down the coast, beach houses are going for $15,000,000.

When the 200-bed prison originally opened in 1959, it likely was more isolated since there was very little development in the area. From 1883 till 1958, it was the quarantine station for immigrants arriving in Canada. During World War I, it was also used as a training centre for the Chinese Labour Corps, which was a force of workers the British Government recruited to perform manual labour to help free troops for front-line duty. There are good views of the prison from Weirs Beach. Once a year, the prison opens its doors to the public. The institution runs the only prison theatre company in all of Canada, and every December for the last 33 years, they have been creating plays that the public are invited to experience.

Address 6000 William Head Road, BC V9C 0B5, best viewed from adjacent beach |
Getting there Bus 54, 55 to William Head Institution | Hours Unlimited from adjacent
beach | Tip Pearson College is Canada's most International school and the country's only
World International College, with students from 150 countries. The views from the rustic
oceanfront campus are beautiful (650 Pearson College Drive, www.pearsoncollege.ca).

107 __ Willows Galley Fish & Chips

Love shack

Willows Galley Fish & Chips is not only an authentic neighbourhood chippy with good quality nosh, but it also has a unique back history that infuses your meal with a dash of love. Owners Dave and Jennifer Higgins had their first date here many years ago. After years running another fish-and-chip shop in Oak Bay, the couple returned to this spot in 2011, and now they side by side, resurrecting the same house-made menu that first brought them together.

The shop itself has been here since 1980, which makes it a contender for historic building status in one's heart, if not in reality. The menu, however, is fully up to date. There is more than "just" fish and chips. You can get panko-breaded oysters, prawns, and scallops, and if you like all those options, you can order the Davy Jones burger, which includes all three topped with tartar sauce and coleslaw! There's a traditional hamburger on the menu, but why not expand your repertoire and try the pulled pork sandwich served with Swiss cheese and apple slaw on a kaiser bun? Or try one of the three types of *poutine*.

Ordering is as fun as eating. Menu items have great names, like The Beachcomber, The Buccaneer, The Neptune, and The Treasure Chest. On a chilly day order the chilli, or a bowl of chowder. On a sunny day, stop by for an ice cream or a milkshake. There are picnic benches outside. All of Willows' packaging is recyclable so don't think twice about getting your fish to-go.

Willows Beach itself is just a five-minute walk away, and you can also stroll through the Estevan Village shopping area. A few blocks away at 256 Heron Street you'll find the oldest building in Oak Bay: Tod House. It was built in 1850 by Hudson Bay Company trader John Tod, and it remains a private residence.

Address 2559 Estevan Avenue, Victoria, BC V8R 2S8, +1 (250) 598-2711, www.willowsgalley.com | Getting there Bus 5 to Estevan at Dunlevy | Hours Wed–Sun noon–6pm | Tip Bungalow in Estevan Village is a great shop to visit and find something unique for your home (2525 Estevan Avenue, www.bungalowgift.ca).

108 Woo the Monkey Muse
An artist finds her kindred spirit

Everyone knows Emily Carr (1871–1945) was a great Canadian painter, but did you know she had a pet monkey? Look closely at the bronze statue of Carr, located halfway between the Empress Hotel and the Legislature Buildings, and you'll notice it includes said monkey on her shoulder. Meet Woo. The Javanese macaque monkey was adopted by Carr in 1923 and, by all accounts, was a greater friend to her than Bubbles was to Michael Jackson. She painted two portraits of Woo, and many sketches. And, like Jackson and Bubbles, Carr even took Woo with her on her travels.

Carr first met Woo at the Bird and Pet Shop on Government Street. She was very fond of animals and had a variety of pets, including parrots, chipmunks, a raccoon, white rats, cats, and several dogs. If you look down from Carr's shoulders to her feet you'll see her bobtail sheepdog Billie, who accompanied her on painting expeditions to Haida Gwaii, the Queen Charlotte Islands, and many of the other locations that the artist immortalised. But her relationship with Woo was the most exceptional – definitely the most unusual – of her animal friends and lasted until 1937. During their first night together, the monkey cooed, "Woo woo woo," and that's why she's called Woo. Some people call her "Mr. Woo," but she was indeed a female. That's why Carr made her short, wide dresses of wool or heavy cotton with a thick canvas apron worn over top. Carr also fixed Woo up with a nice pink tutu. Unfortunately, Woo chewed off all the buttons, so Carr had to design belts and buckles to close up at the back. Woo was a rascal and not only chewed buttons, but also ate some of Carr's paints. So, while it's true Woo was in some of Carr's paintings and sketches, it is also true that some of Carr's paint was in Woo too.

The *Emily Carr* statue by artist Barbara Paterson was unveiled during Women's History Month in 2010.

Address Government & Belleville Streets, Victoria, BC V8W 1W5, www.tourismvictoria.com | **Getting there** Bus 30, 31, 75 to Legislature Terminal at Belleville Street | **Hours** Unrestricted | **Tip** Look for the mural of Emily and Woo on the Quadra Street side of the Island Blue Art & Framing store nearby (905 Fort Street).

109 World War II Radio Tower

Concrete cupcake at the top of Mt. Douglas

There's a bizarre, cupcake-looking cement feature at the top of PKOLS/ Mount Douglas. It is all that is left of a 30-foot-tall VHF/DF radio direction-finding station system that was built here during World War II. The 1969 movie *The Battle of Britain* featured VHF radio as part of an integrated fighter control system that allowed data from a number of sources to be gathered and analysed at a central location so that Spitfires could be efficiently directed toward invading Nazi aircraft. It was essentially the same story here.

During World War II, the Royal Canadian Air Force adopted elements of this control system to build this station and at least two others. (There are remnants of a station at Point No Point and a much smaller hexagon base on Radar Hill near Tofino.) The wooden tower that stood over this concrete cupcake has since been dismantled, but it would have looked a bit like a small windmill without the rotating blades. Inside would have been a radio antenna and a radio operator sitting below it. Today, what you see is the base, modified in the 1960s to include a bench, and a brass medallion that shows distances to the various land features you can see from here.

Surrounding the cupcake is a whopping 464 acres of land and has 21 kilometres (13 miles) of trails that take you through the largest urban forest on the Saanich Peninsula. The trails will lead you through the forest, around the base of the summit, up to the spectacular view at the mountain summit or down to the secluded, sandy beach. Keep an eye out for herons, wildflowers, cedars, and fish in the creek. Also look for the elevation and distance markers. Take the 1,500-metre (1-mile) hike from the Churchill parking lot gate to the Summit parking lot for a 160-metre (525-foot) change in elevation.

Address 4500 Cedar Hill Road, Victoria, BC V8X 3S8, +1 (250) 475-5522, www.saanich.ca, parks@saanich.ca | Getting there Bus 39 to Shelbourne at Robinwood | Hours Unrestricted hiking; Summit access daily noon–10pm, gates locked at 11pm | Tip Cormorant Point is another place worth scampering around. See if you can find the abandoned blockhouse that looks like a saltwater swimming pool (staircase at the north end of Balmacarra Road, Saanich, www.coastview.org/2022/02/19/cormorant-point-gordon-head).

110 World's Tallest Totem Pole

This is the free-standing one

The world's tallest totem pole is almost 38 metres (127 feet) tall. Its massive height makes it easy to find near the southeast corner of Beacon Hill Park, where it towers majestically over Juan de Fuca Strait. The pole, erected in 1956, was carved by a team led by Mungo Martin, the Kwakiutl tribal chief. Before you can carve a totem pole, you must find a suitable tree. This one came from a 3,600-acre stand of trees in the Sooke region, and it was a real beauty. The 40.5-metre (133-foot) cedar was the straightest and tallest tree to be found at that time. After it was delimbed and cut down, it was pushed and dragged into Muir Creek and then towed behind an old tugboat into the Victoria Inner Harbour.

Most people don't realise that the average lifespan of a totem pole is a mere 50 years. Just like old wooden homes, they need to be maintained. Over its lifespan, this one has been painted four times and has had various other refurbishments. In July of 2000, the totem pole had decayed to the point where it needed to be taken down and totally restored. Through the hard work of many community volunteers and under the skilled supervision of Coast Salish artist Master Seaman Vern Point, the pole was restored to its former glory and erected again in November of 2001. Eventually, the pole will no longer be viable though, at which time, in keeping with tradition, it will be returned to the earth to decompose and nurture the growth of new trees for future generations.

There is another totem pole northeast of Vancouver Island at Alert Bay on Cormorant Island that is technically taller. It stands at 52.7 metres (173 feet) tall, but it has several guide wires attached to the ground that hold it in place. It is also carved from not one but two pieces of timber. The totem pole in Beacon Park is the world's tallest *free standing* totem pole.

Address Beacon Hill Park, 100 Cook Street, Victoria, BC V8V 0B9, www.victoria.ca/EN/main/
residents/parks/beacon-hill/story-pole.html | Getting there Bus 3 to Dallas at Washington, or
bus 2, 3, 5 to Douglas at Avalon | Hours Unrestricted | Tip Stroll over to see a 5.1-metre-tall
(17-foot), grey, stainless steel, garden watering can, an impressive piece of art, installed in 2007,
that has been sprinkling people with its array of surprising water jets every summer since then
(Beacon Hill Park near the corner of Circle Drive & Park Way, www.crd.bc.ca/landmarks/artwork).

111 Zodiac Crosswalk

No zebras allowed on this crossing

There are many ways to celebrate a new year. Drinking champagne, kissing a loved one at midnight, and enjoying a firework display are the typical Western ways to do it. Celebrating Chinese New Year is done much the same way: sharing a meal with family, setting off fireworks, exchanging gifts, and maybe watching a lion and dragon dance. But when the Year of the Tiger arrived in 2022, Victoria decided to do something different. They decided to mark the occasion by painting the pedestrian crosswalk at the intersection of Government and Fisgard Streets with characters from the Chinese zodiac. So, when you stand at the corner and look down, you'll see no "zebra crossing" white stripes, but rather a zoo of animals: rat, ox, tiger, rabbit, dragon, snake, horse, goat, monkey, rooster, dog, and pig.

In the Chinese calendar system, every year has one of the twelve animals assigned to it, meaning each animal comes around again every twelve years. So, for example, the next year of the Tiger will be in 2034. Along with the animal comes a variety of characteristics and predictions. It is said that people born in the year of the Tiger are brave, competitive, unpredictable, and confident. They are also very charming and well-liked by others. On the other hand, they can sometimes be impetuous, irritable, and overindulgent. When crossing the road, none of these characteristics seem very helpful. Better to be patient and cautious, and to look both ways.

When you stand at the northeast corner of this intersection, you'll get a great view of the crosswalk. Across the way, you'll also see the visually remarkable Gate of Harmonious Interest. Walk a few steps beyond the gate to 555 Fisgard, and you'll be at the place where Chinese statesman Tang Hua Lung was assassinated by Chong Wong in 1918. Walk a few steps further, and you'll find the famous and photogenic Fan Tan Alley.

Address Government & Fisgard Streets, Victoria, BC V8W 1Z4 | Getting there Bus 14, 15, 24, 25 to Pandora at Government/Store | Hours Unrestricted | Tip Visit the nearby Chinese Canadian Museum, which aims to tell the story of the Chinese Canadian experience and to "foster respect, inclusion, and collaboration among all communities and across generations" (10–14 Fan Tan Alley, www.chinesecanadianmuseum.ca).

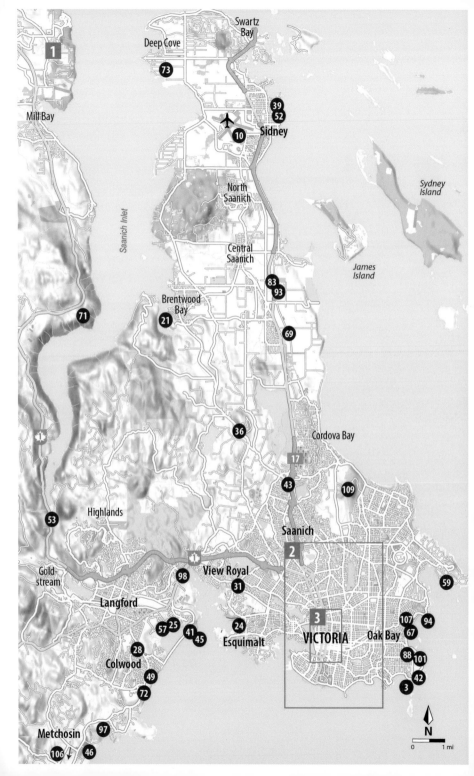

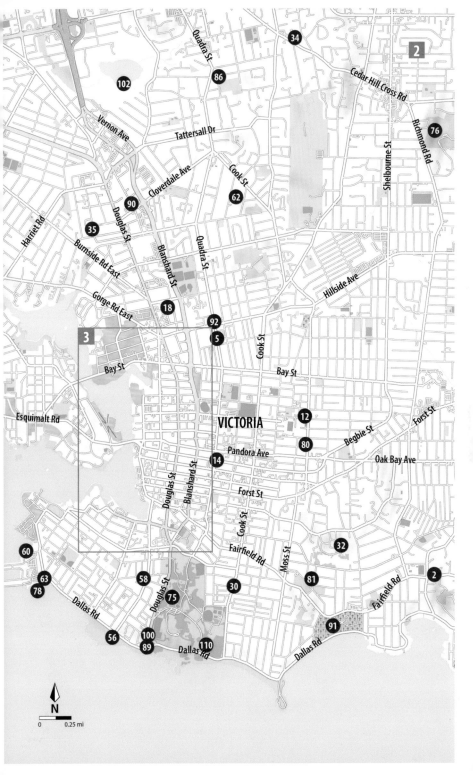

Dave Doroghy, Graeme Menzies
111 Places in Vancouver
That You Must Not Miss
ISBN 978-3-7408-0494-7

Dave Doroghy, Graeme Menzies
111 Places in Whistler
That You Must Not Miss
ISBN 978-3-7408-1046-7

Jennifer Bain, Liz Beddall
111 Places in Ottawa
That You Must Not Miss
ISBN 978-3-7408-1388-8

Jennifer Bain, Christina Ryan
111 Places in Calgary
That You Must Not Miss
ISBN 978-3-7408-0749-8

Elizabeth Lenell-Davies,
Anita Genua, Claire Davenport
111 Places in Toronto
That You Must Not Miss
ISBN 978-3-7408-0257-8

Harriet Baskas, Cortney Kelley
111 Places in Seattle
That You Must Not Miss
ISBN 978-3-7408-1992-7

Katrina Nattress, Jason Quigley
111 Places in Portland
That You Must Not Miss
ISBN 978-3-7408-0750-4

Floriana Petersen, Steve Werney
111 Places in San Francisco
That You Must Not Miss
ISBN 978-3-7408-1698-8

Floriana Petersen, Steve Werney
111 Places in Silicon Valley
That You Must Not Miss
ISBN 978-3-7408-1346-8

Laurel Moglen, Julia Posey,
Lyudmila Zotova
**111 Places in Los Angeles
That You Must Not Miss**
ISBN 978-3-7408-1889-0

Brian Joseph
**111 Places in Hollywood
That You Must Not Miss**
ISBN 978-3-7408-1819-7

Kelsey Roslin, Nic Yeager,
Jesse Pitzler
**111 Places in Austin
That You Must Not Miss**
ISBN 978-3-7408-1642-1

Dana DuTerroil, Joni Fincham,
Daniel Jackson
**111 Places in Houston
That You Must Not Miss**
ISBN 978-3-7408-1697-1

Dana DuTerroil, Joni Fincham,
Sara S. Murphy
**111 Places for Kids in Houston
That You Must Not Miss**
ISBN 978-3-7408-1372-7

Philip D. Armour, Susie Inverso
**111 Places in Denver
That You Must Not Miss**
ISBN 978-3-7408-1220-1

Cristyle Egitto, Jakob Takos
**111 Places in Palm Beach
That You Must Not Miss**
ISBN 978-3-7408-1695-7

Brian Hayden, Jesse Pitzler
**111 Places in Buffalo
That You Must Not Miss**
ISBN 978-3-7408-1440-3

Jo-Anne Elikann, Susan Lusk
**111 Places in New York
That You Must Not Miss**
ISBN 978-3-7408-1888-3

Wendy Lubovich, Ed Lefkowicz
111 Museums in New York
That You Must Not Miss
ISBN 978-3-7408-0379-7

Wendy Lubovich, Jean Hodgens
111 Places in the Hamptons
That You Must Not Miss
ISBN 978-3-7408-1891-3

Kim Windyka, Heather Kapplow,
Alyssa Wood
111 Places in Boston
That You Must Not Miss
ISBN 978-3-7408-1558-5

Andréa Seiger, John Dean
111 Places in Washington
That You Must Not Miss
ISBN 978-3-7408-1890-6

Brandon Schultz, Lucy Baber
111 Places in Philadelphia
That You Must Not Miss
ISBN 978-3-7408-1376-5

Allison Robicelli, John Dean
111 Places in Baltimore
That You Must Not Miss
ISBN 978-3-7408-1696-4

Amy Bizzarri, Susie Inverso
111 Places in Chicago
That You Must Not Miss
ISBN 978-3-7408-1030-6

Michelle Madden, Janet McMillan
111 Places in Milwaukee
That You Must Not Miss
ISBN 978-3-7408-1643-8

Sandra Gurvis, Mitch Geiser
111 Places in Columbus
That You Must Not Miss
ISBN 978-3-7408-0600-2